First Century Early Martyrs

FIRST CENTURY
EARLY MARTYRS

E. MARY CHRISTIE

Angelus Press

PO Box 217 | Saint Marys, KS 66536

Library of Congress Control Number: 2024052138

Scriptural references taken from the Douay-Rheims Catholic Bible.

Artwork Credits
Roman Provinces around the time of Jesus. User:Andrein, "Roman Empire 125", https://creativecommons.org/licenses/by-sa/3.0/legalcode

Israel at the time of Jesus. Library of Congress Geography and Map Division

ANGELUS PRESS
PO Box 217
St. Marys, Kansas 66536-0217
Phone (816) 753-3150
FAX (816) 753-3557
Order Line 1-800-966-7337
www.angeluspress.org

ISBN: 978-1-68529-088-7
FIRST PRINTING–December 2024

Printed in the United States of America

Contents

Roman Provinces around the time of Jesus

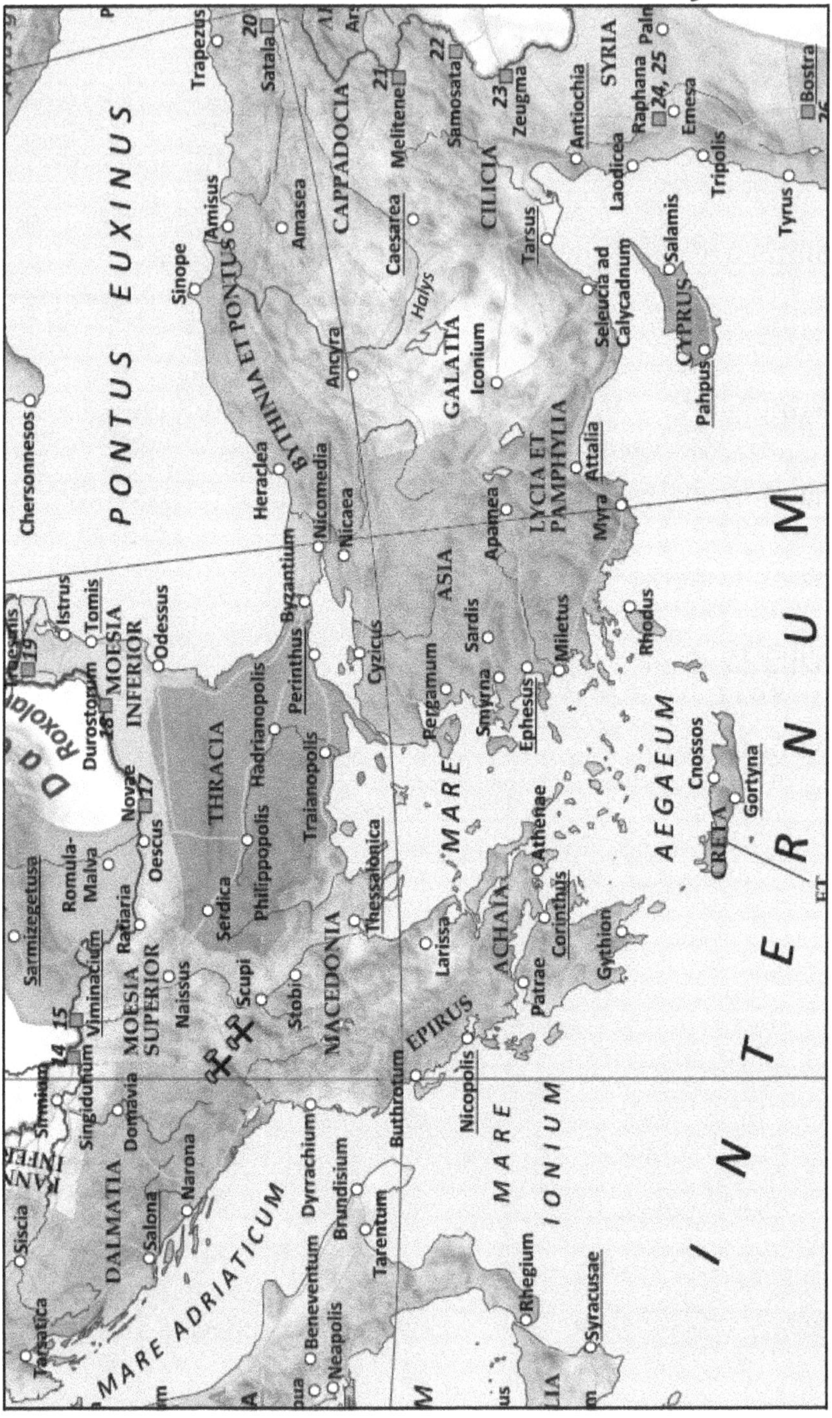

Israel at the time of Jesus

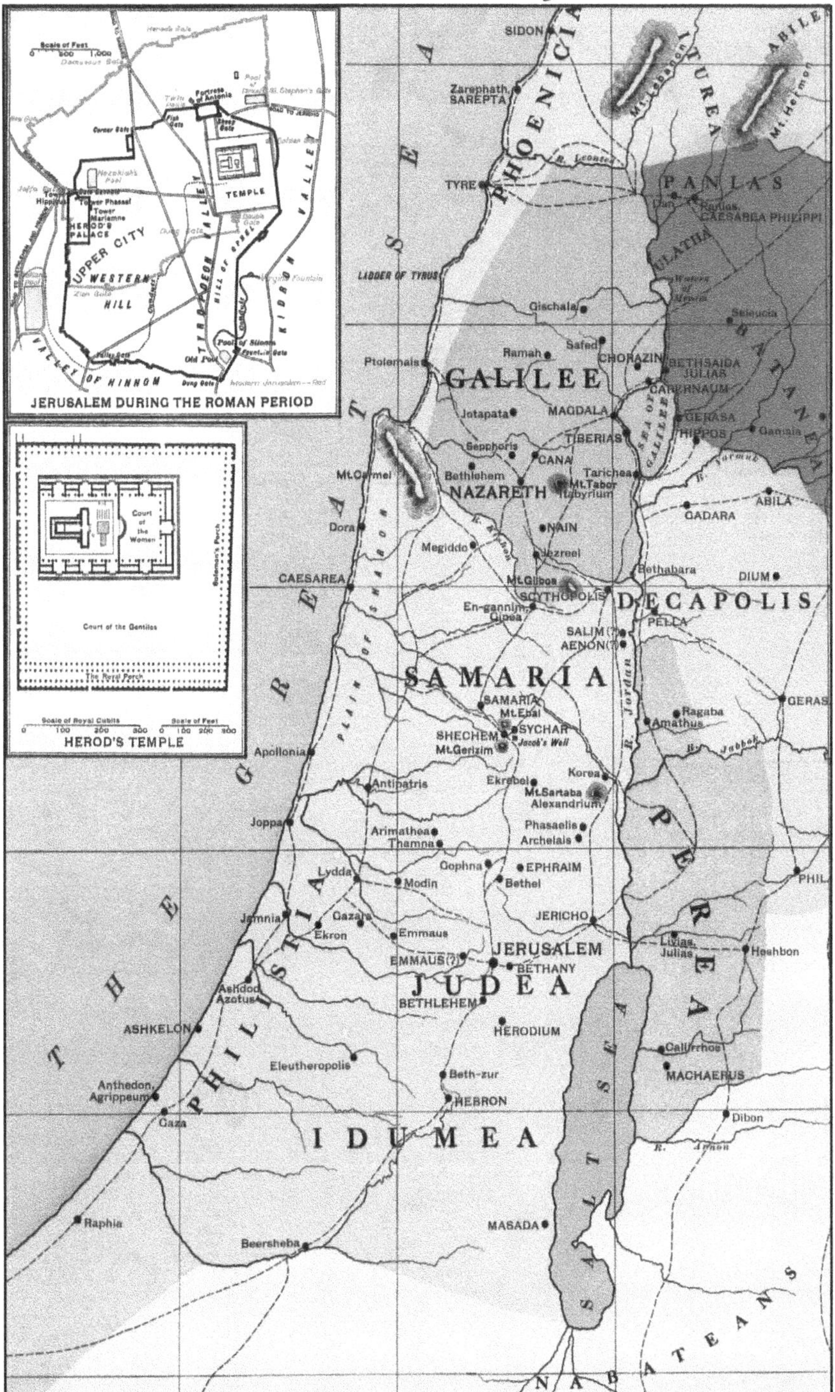

Summary

Further to the author's tour of the Holy Gospels detailing the lives of the Twelve Apostles (each of whom, aside from John, died a martyr's death), this book now seeks to provide an insightful study into the life and character of each of the remaining six Early Martyrs who also suffered a holy martyrdom in the first century.

The first three—Stephen, Mark, and Barnabas—were blessed to have been well-acquainted with Jesus, His Blessed Virgin Mother, and the Apostles, and will be seen to have enjoyed a strong friendship, bonded together as devout Early Christians, deeply devoted to their beloved Jesus and His Mother; in due time becoming early disciples, boldly preaching Christ's gospel message throughout the then-known world.

The other three—Timothy, Paul, and Luke—never met Our Lord (having converted after Christ's Ascension), but once converted, they too became devout early disciples of Christ, united as good friends in their apostolic calling.

As we examine the life and character of each of these Early Martyrs, may their various virtues, molded on the infinite holiness of their divine Master, inspire us to follow their saintly example—and may their courageous stand in the defense of the one, true Faith that Jesus Christ taught (handed down through His Twelve and the Early Church) inspire us to never give up the good fight.

Saint Stephen
(5 AD—34 AD)

CHAPTER 1

Saint Stephen

December 26

Saint Stephen, renowned for his piety and courage, was the first of the Early Christians to be martyred—his bold defense of Jesus as the Messiah resulted in his being stoned to death (believed to have occurred in 34 AD).

History dictates that our Saint was a Greek-speaking Jew, born in Jerusalem in 5 AD.

While we have no information as to when Stephen became a follower of Christ, given that he was an inhabitant of Jerusalem it may well have been during Christ's early ministry. Not long after performing His first public miracle (at the wedding feast of Cana),[1] we know that Jesus traveled to Jerusalem with His Mother and first chosen Apostles[2] to celebrate the Jewish Pasch. At this time, upon entering the Temple, Jesus found oxen, sheep, and doves being sold in this holy place of worship and promptly drove them out of "*the house of my Father*"[3]—which no doubt attracted much attention.

Indeed, in light of God having deigned our Saint to become an Early Christian, Stephen may well have witnessed the money-changers fleeing the Temple, surrounded by droves of oxen and sheep,

[1] Jn. 2:1-11.

[2] Seven fishermen: Peter, Andrew, James, John, Philip, Bartholomew, and Thomas.

[3] Jn. 2:13-16.

and in his typically bold way, would have been drawn to investigate what was going on. Upon entering God's holy place of worship, now cleansed of the sellers and their merchandise, he would have witnessed Jesus (surrounded by His Apostles) miraculously healing the blind and the lame who happened to be there at the time[4]—no doubt leaving Stephen overawed, and determined to know more about this holy Man of God.

Following this train of thought, we can imagine Stephen boldly approaching the Apostles, who would have willingly brought him to their Master—and upon sensing the wondrous joy of Christ's divine presence, our twenty-five-year-old Saint would have instantly felt a strong desire to become one of Christ's devoted followers.

Furthermore, as the widowed mother of the evangelist Mark owned a large house in Jerusalem (believed to have been the size of a monastery) where Jesus, His Blessed Mother, and the Apostles lived whenever they visited the city,[5] we can imagine Stephen being invited into the home of Mark's mother that very same day, where he would have met the Blessed Virgin Mary, along with Mark (eighteen years old at the time) and his mother (and at some point Mark's thirty-year-old cousin, the disciple Barnabas). And having met Christ's holy Mother, inevitably Stephen would have been drawn to her quiet saintly presence, filled as she was with every grace and heavenly virtue—further inspiring our Saint to never want to leave the holy group.

Quite possibly Stephen may have remained in the home of Mark's mother—in due time becoming the best of friends with Mark and Barnabas. Thus we can imagine the three of them accompanying their beloved Blessed Virgin Mary, Mark's mother, and other Holy Women, following Jesus and His Apostles whenever possible throughout the three years of His divine ministry; eagerly listening

---

4 Matt. 21:14.

5 Acts 1:13; 12:12.

and learning from their divine Master's preachings, and marveling over His many wondrous miracles—their love for Christ and faith in all that He taught uniting them as devoted followers.

Then when Jesus brought His Apostles to Jerusalem for what He knew would be the last time that He would be celebrating the Jewish Pasch, while Mark's mother and other Holy Women would have been helping the Blessed Virgin Mary to prepare her Son's last Pascal meal, it is easy to envisage Stephen helping his dear friends Mark and Barnabas (under the Virgin Mary's careful instructions) to set up a refectory table with the required seating in the large upper room in the home of Mark's mother where Jesus had chosen to celebrate His Last Supper, alone with His Apostles.

Once Jesus arrived at the house and began celebrating His Last Supper with the Twelve, we can further imagine Stephen, Mark, and Barnabas in another room dining with their Blessed Virgin Mary, Mark's mother, and other Holy Women—at which time the Virgin Mary may well have shared with them that which she knew was taking place in the other room, that her Son was telling His Apostles that He would soon be returning to His Father in Heaven.[6] Wide-eyed, all would have greeted the news as they pondered on the meaning of their beloved Virgin Mary's words. And in her gentle, loving way, Christ's holy Mother would have led her loved ones in prayer to the Eternal Father (her courageous trust in His holy Will later seen to have inspired Stephen, Mark, and Barnabas to follow her saintly example).

After Christ's Last Supper had ended, no doubt the group quietly watched from an upper window as their divine Master followed by His Apostles stepped away from the house into the darkness of the night—and once He was gone from sight, the Virgin Mary would once again have led her loved ones in prayer to the Eternal Father.

---

[6] Jn. 16:28.

The hours that followed would have been long, drawn out, and painful, with little sleep for any of them. Come morning, Stephen would have learned that the Blessed Virgin Mary and Apostle John had left the house very early, concerned to know what had happened to their beloved Jesus. Along with Mark and Barnabas and the rest of the household, our Saint would have anxiously awaited news—only to later discover that Jesus had been betrayed by Judas Iscariot; unjustly arrested; viciously scourged; blasphemously mocked; brutally crowned with a ring of thorns; made to carry a heavy Cross; and then savagely crucified on Calvary's hilltop, where three hours later their infinitely merciful Good Shepherd gave up His life for His sheep. It isn't difficult to visualize the horrified looks on the face of all who received the news (clearly our saintly Stephen, as later revealed, resolved to stand up against those who refused to believe that Jesus was Christ the Messiah, and in their savage revolt had crucified his beloved Good Shepherd and Master).

Now on the third day after Christ's Crucifixion and Burial, we can readily picture Stephen with Mark and Barnabas, persevering in prayer with their Christian brethren in the home of Mark's mother, when a little later that same morning Mary Magdalen came sobbing to their Apostle friends Peter and John saying that she had left the house very early (along with other Holy Women) and upon arrival at Christ's tomb had found the great stone rolled away from its entrance, and the Body of their Jesus no longer inside.[7]

In contemplating the occasion, Stephen along with Mark and Barnabas would have noticed Peter and John promptly depart from the house—returning an hour or so later confirming that they too had found the tomb to be empty.[8] Even as all received the news feeling somewhat troubled, Mary Magdalen (who had quietly followed the Apostles when they had left the house) came bursting through

---

[7] Jn. 20:1-3.
[8] Jn. 20:3-10.

the door, now excitedly claiming that after Peter and John had left the tomb, she beheld a man standing near her by the entrance. Thinking him to be the gardener, she asked if he knew where the Body of Jesus had been laid, but the Man responded by addressing her by name—whereupon she promptly recognized His voice as that of Jesus.[9] However, most of the household were not convinced[10] (thinking that in her emotional state, the Magdalen must have been imagining these things), when a little later that same day, two disciples then arrived at the house, also claiming to have seen Jesus—their words similarly greeted with disbelief (although not by Stephen, Mark, and Barnabas, who we can imagine quietly discussing the exciting news with their dear friends Peter and John).[11]

Not long afterwards we know that Jesus then suddenly appeared before the household[12]—inviting those who did not believe to touch His hands and His feet that they may believe that He was not a ghost but had truly risen as He had said He would. And with what joy all received Him![13]

Thereafter, once it was time for their Risen Christ to ascend into Heaven, we can readily picture Stephen, Mark, and Barnabas accompanying their beloved Blessed Virgin Mary, Mark's dear mother, and other Holy Women as they quietly walked up Mount Olivet following their Apostle friends, no doubt feeling deeply saddened to meet their Risen Christ on the summit for the last time. And once assembled on the hilltop, when Jesus miraculously appeared, after reiterating His instructions to His Apostles to go forth and preach

---

[9] Jn. 20:14-17.

[10] Mk. 16:11-13.

[11] And nor, indeed, did the Blessed Virgin Mary have doubt—for pious belief, upheld by no less than six Doctors of the Church (including Sts. Ambrose, Anselm, and Albert the Great) holds that Jesus had first appeared to His beloved Mother while she was praying alone in her room.

[12] Lk. 24:36-40.

[13] Jn. 20:20.

His gospel to all nations,[14] we know that He bid His beloved Mother and all His dear faithful a tender farewell, gently consoling them with His sweet promise that He would always be with them "*even to the consummation of the world.*"[15]

Yet in spite of these comforting words, as Jesus lifted Himself up and slowly ascended into the Heavens above, we can imagine Stephen and everyone else feeling a deep sense of sadness as they kept their eyes fixed on their beloved Jesus until a cloud hid Him from sight. However, we know that God sent down two angels who now appeared before them arrayed in white garments,[16] assuring them that "*this Jesus who is taken up from you into Heaven, shall so come, as you have seen Him going into Heaven.*" Clearly comforted, on their arrival back in Jerusalem we know that everyone joyfully gathered in the home of Mark's mother, where over the days that followed they all persevered in prayer with the Blessed Virgin Mary and Apostles.[17]

Now not long after Christ's Ascension, Stephen would still have been with his dear friends Mark and Barnabas, along with other Christian brethren (some one hundred and twenty) when Peter (in his role as Prince of the Apostles) called upon them to help elect a Twelfth Apostle to replace Judas[18]—at which time we know that Matthias was chosen.

Thereafter, there occurred the miracle of Pentecost; no doubt Stephen, Mark, and Barnabas gathered with their Christian brethren in the home of Mark's mother (which had already become a popular meeting place)—when that mighty wind resounded throughout the whole house[19] (heralding the arrival of the Holy Ghost, the Paraclete). Albeit somewhat alarmed, the group would have quickly

---

[14] Mt. 28:19.
[15] Mt. 28:20.
[16] Acts 1:10-11.
[17] Acts 1:13-14.
[18] Acts 1:15-26.
[19] Acts 2:1-4.

learned that upstairs (in that same large upper room where Jesus had celebrated His Last Supper), while the Blessed Virgin Mary and Apostles were praying together, the wondrous miracle of the Holy Ghost had descended over each one of them (in the form of parted tongues of fire) filling them with His heavenly gifts (to include enabling the Apostles to speak in divers tongues).

Thus endowed, the Apostles (commencing with Peter's famous homily to the great crowd that had assembled outside their home)[20] preached in the Temple daily, converting many souls—promptly inspiring Stephen (along with Mark and Barnabas) to follow their saintly example. And before too long, when Peter and John approached the Temple at the ninth hour of prayer one day, a lame man called out to them begging for alms.[21] In light of the Apostles having no money, Peter reached down and took hold of the man's right hand, saying: "*In the name of Jesus Christ of Nazareth, arise, and walk*"—whereupon the man leapt up, promptly healed of his infirmity.

Yet even as Stephen and his friends rejoicingly gave glory to God, the elders and high priests were filled with envy as they watched the number of Christians continuing to grow (some five thousand already)—and now sought to silence the Apostles.[22] Not that they were successful, for Peter was able to argue with them in a way that left them unable to dispute his words—nor indeed find a plausible reason to have them locked away. So Peter and John and the other Apostles continued to follow the example of their courageous Good Shepherd, preaching His gospel throughout the city.

And as the number of converts continued to grow, in order to help with their apostolic work, Peter called upon the brethren to

---

[20] Acts 2:5-41 (at which time some three thousand were converted and baptized).

[21] Acts 3:1-8.

[22] Acts 4:4-21.

seek out seven men of good reputation, full of the Holy Ghost and wisdom.[23]

Now as our saintly Stephen by this time was reputed to be blessed with heavenly wisdom and a strong faith in all that Christ taught, the Apostles chose him, along with six others,[24] and ordained them as deacons (no doubt the news filling Mark and Barnabas with admiration for their beloved brother in Christ). Furthermore, aside from helping to distribute food and charitable aid to the poorer members of the Christian community (in particular the Greek-speaking Jewish widows who at the time were being neglected), Stephen was also called upon to help the Apostles minister to the faithful—where, in his elected role, our Saint unwittingly found fame.[25] For filled as he was with the necessary graces and fortitude, he performed great wonders and miracles, and converted many souls.

Alas it wasn't long before the seed of envy once again arose among those not of the Christian community. Having failed to match Stephen's heavenly wisdom they reported him to the Sanhedrin[26]—and like they did to Christ before the same council, they accused Stephen of blasphemy, claiming that he spoke against the holy place and their Mosaic law, and they even produced witnesses who gave false testimony, saying:[27]

"This man ceaseth not to speak words against the holy place and the law. For we have heard him say, that this Jesus of Nazareth shall destroy this place, and shall change the traditions which Moses delivered unto us."

Yet after they had brutally arrested Stephen and brought him before the Sanhedrin, the elders murmured amongst themselves for

---

23 Acts 6:1-3.

24 The other six being Philip, Prochorus, Nicanor, Timon, Parmenas, and Nicolas.

25 Acts 6:8.

26 The supreme legal court made up of Jewish elders.

27 Acts 6:12-14.

in spite of the vicious treatment and false allegations being leveled against their accused, he appeared not at all perturbed; in fact, they thought they were seeing the face of an angel.[28] Prompted to hear what he had to say, the elders allowed our Saint to speak—whereupon (blessed as he was with the gifts of the Holy Ghost) Stephen spoke to them fearlessly and at some length.

He refuted the lies that he had blasphemed by outlining his belief in all that the ancients taught concerning their fathers.[29] He also spoke of Moses, born in Egypt during the time of Pharaoh's persecution of the Israelites (their own family tree), where this evil king was using their menfolk as slaves and treating them most cruelly.[30]

Going further, Stephen told them how God saved the life of Moses that he may lead His Chosen People out of their bondage—reminding the elders how the God of their fathers (the God of Abraham, the God of Isaac, and the God of Jacob) had spoken to Moses through the flame of a burning bush.[31]

He then went on to remind the elders that after leaving Egypt, in spite of God working great wonders and signs throughout their sojourn in the desert (towards the Promised Land) and God speaking to Moses on Mount Sinai providing him with the "*words of life*" (God's Ten Commandments), their fathers disobeyed God by creating an idol in the image of a calf which they chose to worship as their god.[32] And knowing as Stephen did that the elders continued to refute the teachings of Jesus, the Just One, he courageously went on to point out their infidelity by telling them:

"You stiff-necked and uncircumcised in heart and ears, you always resist the Holy Ghost: as your fathers did, so do you also. Which of the prophets have not your fathers persecuted? And they have slain them who

---

28 Acts 6:15.
29 Acts 7:1-19.
30 Acts 7:19-29.
31 Acts 7:30-41.
32 Acts 7:51-53.

foretold of the coming of the Just One; of whom you have been now the betrayers and murderers: who have received the Law by the disposition of angels, and have not kept it."

At our Saint's bold admonishment, the elders were now enraged.[33] Yet even as the air throbbed with their fury the Holy Ghost suddenly gave to Stephen a miraculous heavenly vision. Pointing upwards, our Saint stalwartly told them:[34]

"*Behold, I see the Heavens opened, and the Son of Man standing on the right hand of God!*"

Alas, rather than being convinced, this only served to enrage the elders even further. Gnashing their teeth, they blocked their ears, refusing to hear another word.[35] With one accord they violently grabbed dear Stephen, and dragging him through the streets they cast him forth from the city gates—where they proceeded to viciously stone him.

Yet undeterred in his great love for the Messiah and aware of his divine Master's merciful words while being nailed to the Cross,[36] as the heavy stones brought our Saint to his knees, he cried out to his good Lord God:[37]

"Lord, lay not this sin to their charge."

Shortly thereafter, in the midst of the flying rocks pounding against his fallen body, God's faithful disciple at the tender age of twenty-nine "*fell asleep in the Lord.*"

Once Mark and Barnabas heard what happened, they clearly felt determined to follow in the bold footsteps of their heroic friend (as later revealed herein).

Promptly after Stephen's martyrdom, in order to save their disciples from the great persecution that had now been unleashed against

---

[33] Acts 7:54.
[34] Acts 7:55.
[35] Acts 7:56-57.
[36] Lk. 23:34.
[37] Acts 7:59.

the Early Church in Jerusalem,[38] the Apostles sent a good number of them away from the city into Judea, Samaria, and elsewhere (although not Barnabas and Mark at this time)—the stoning of our beloved Saint seen to have sparked the spread of Christianity throughout the then-known world. Meanwhile, the Apostles themselves, inspired by their saintly deacon's warrior stand in the defense of Christ, bravely remained in the city for a time, determined to reinforce the roots of Christ's holy Church.

For centuries the location of Stephen's tomb was not known—until late 415 AD when a priest known as Fr. Lucian learned by revelation that our Saint's body had been buried in Caphargamala, a place some distance to the north of Jerusalem. His relics were promptly exhumed and carried to the Church of Mount Sion in Jerusalem, where they remained until transferred in 460 AD to St. Stephen's Basilica—a new church built in honor of our Saint outside the Damascus Gate (the main gate along the northern wall of the city) over the spot where his stoning had taken place.

It is clear from St. Stephen's courageous, outspoken defense of the Messiah that (like the Apostles) he was deeply inspired by the exemplary courage of their divine Master—and that of His holy Mother who had stalwartly stood at the foot of the Cross surrounded by blasphemous abuses being hurled at her beloved Son by the chief priests, scribes and ancients (as revealed to our Saint by his good friend John, who we know had remained right by the Virgin Mary's side).

May such exemplary courage inspire us to remain true to the traditional sacred precepts of the one, true Church[39] that Jesus Christ instituted upon the earth—even when we ourselves are faced with scorn and persecution.

---

[38] Acts 8:1.

[39] Christ's One, Holy, Catholic, Apostolic Church (the traditional holy Roman Catholic Church, recognizable by its Four Marks).

Saint Mark
(12 AD—68 AD)

CHAPTER 2

Saint Mark

April 25

Saint Mark (also known as John or John Mark[40]), like his dear friend Stephen, in due time also became a most devout and courageous disciple; his lionhearted devotion to Christ not only resulting in his becoming known as the "*Lionhearted*"—but similarly earning him a holy martyrdom (believed to have occurred in 68 AD).

Tradition dictates that Mark was born in 12 AD in the city of Cyrene[41] to wealthy parents (Aristopolos and Mary), Jewish descendants of the tribe of Levi,[42] and was a cousin of the disciple Barnabas.[43]

Not only was our Saint related to Barnabas, but his father Aristopolos was related to the Apostle Peter's mother-in-law. In light of this family connection, we can imagine Mark's parents attending Peter's wedding in Bethsaida, Galilee (at which time Mark was just an infant). While they were away, Tradition dictates that their home in Cyrene was attacked and destroyed, whereupon Mark's wealthy

---

40 Acts 12:12 and 25.

41 In biblical times, Ancient Cyrene was located on the coast of North Africa at the site of modern-day Shahhat, Libya. It was the most important of the five Greek cities in the region known as the Pentapolis.

42 The tribe of Levi, traditionally descended from the Israelite Levi (son of Jacob, descendant of Aaron, first high priest of Israel) were assigned particular religious duties (and had political responsibilities as well).

43 Col. 4:10.

parents then migrated to Galilee and settled in Cana (a small village at the time)—within easy traveling distance to Peter's family.

Some years later, young Mark and his mother suffered the loss of Mark's father, whereupon Peter (who had no children of his own and was possibly already a widower) adopted a fatherly role toward his young relative[44]—and as soon as our Saint reached school age, is believed to have suggested to Mark's mother that she may like to have him schooled in Jerusalem to ensure that he receive a sound education. So Mark's wealthy mother purchased that large house in Jerusalem,[45] whereupon we can imagine Peter (along with his brother Andrew) helping Mark's mother with the move.

Then thirteen years later (just three days after Jesus had called Peter, Andrew, and their fishermen friends to become His *"fishers of men"*)[46] there occurred the famous wedding feast in Cana. Not only were Jesus, His Blessed Virgin Mother, and first-chosen Apostles present, but historical records[47] reveal that our young Saint (by now in his late teens) and his mother were also invited. Upon their arrival we can imagine Peter joyfully introducing his relatives to Jesus, Mary, and the other Apostles—and as Mark had offered to help serve at the feast, his mother apparently sat with the holy group at their table. As readily imagined, it didn't take long before Mark's mother set her heart on becoming a devoted follower of Jesus—and having met the Blessed Virgin Mary, promptly developed a close friendship with Christ's holy Mother (as evidenced by her inviting

---

44 I Pet. 5:13.

45 Many years later, the Monastery of St. Mark was built on the site of Mark's family home in Jerusalem. When the Monastery underwent restoration in 1940, an inscription dating back to the sixth century was found inside the Monastery stating: "*This is the house of Mary, mother of John called Mark. Proclaimed a church by the holy apostles under the name of the Virgin Mary, Mother of God, after the Ascension of our Lord Jesus Christ into Heaven. Renewed after the destruction of Jerusalem by Titus in the year AD 73.*"

46 Mt. 4:19; Mk. 1:17.

47 Historical records maintained by the Early Fathers of the Coptic Church in Egypt (which Church, Saint Mark later founded in Alexandria).

Jesus, the Virgin Mary, and Apostles to live in her house whenever they were in Jerusalem).

Now during the wedding feast we know of course that Jesus performed His first public miracle after His beloved Mother had interceded with Him.[48] As our young Saint helped fill the seven waterpots at Our Lord's request, we can readily imagine his awestruck reaction upon learning that Jesus had miraculously turned the water into wine—and like his mother, promptly opened his heart to Jesus.

Indeed, over time we know that Mark became the first of the evangelists—in his lionhearted way, determined to convert all souls by writing on the life of Christ. And having boldly taken this project under his wing, our Saint is sometimes portrayed in artwork as a man holding a pen and scroll of paper in the company of a winged lion. As this powerfully-built beast is typically known as the "king of beasts," such artwork not only points to the fearlessness of Mark but reminds us of the supernatural strength and power of Christ the King (who reigns over all creation and triumphs over the evil forces of sin).

Once the wedding feast was over, while young Mark and his mother returned to Jerusalem, in light of Peter having adopted a fatherly role towards Mark, he was able to share with our Saint what happened after Jesus, His Mother, and the Apostles had returned to their hometown of Capharnaum[49] (enabling Mark to provide us with the details). Indeed, from Mark's Gospel[50] we learn that on the following Sabbath, Jesus took Peter, Andrew, James, and John into the local synagogue and began preaching to the people—where all listened in astonishment for He "*was teaching them as one having power, and not as the scribes.*" Suddenly there appeared a man who was possessed, screaming at Jesus:

---

48 Jn. 2:3-11.
49 Jn. 2:12.
50 Mk. 1:21-24.

"What have we to do with thee, Jesus of Nazareth? Art thou come to destroy us? I know who thou art, the Holy One of God."

Having performed His first public miracle, Jesus ordered the demonic spirit to depart from the man, whereupon Mark tells us that the demon cried out with a loud voice and departed,[51] leaving the people filled with wonderment (the fame of Our Lord promptly spreading throughout the fishing village and all of Galilee).

Our Saint's Gospel[52] then goes on to reveal that on leaving the synagogue that day, Jesus and His Apostles returned to Peter's family home in Capharnaum (where they were all residing at the time, including Christ's holy Mother). Immediately upon their arrival, the Blessed Virgin Mary (full knowing what her Son would do) greeted them with the news that Peter's mother-in-law had been struck with a high fever and was now seriously ill in bed—whereupon Jesus hurried to her bedside, and gently taking her by the hand, promptly healed her of her illness (leaving all four Apostles once again filled with awe).

After what happened in the synagogue that morning, Mark learned from Peter that after sunset that evening a large crowd suddenly appeared at their door, bringing all who were ill or possessed with devils—and our beloved Jesus healed them all.[53]

Now not long after this eventful day, as the Jewish Pasch was fast approaching[54] (a time when we know families would travel from far away to celebrate this annual feast in Jerusalem), in light of Mark's mother having invited Jesus, His Mother, and the Apostles to live in her house whenever they traveled to the city, we can readily picture our Saint helping his mother to prepare their large home—and oh with what rejoicing they would have welcomed Jesus and His Blessed Mother, along with Peter, Andrew, and the other Apostles.

---

[51] Mk. 1:25-28.
[52] Mk. 1:29-31.
[53] Mk. 1:32-34.
[54] Jn. 2:13.

The following morning, after Jesus had taken His Apostles into the Temple and had discovered oxen, sheep, and doves being sold amidst much furor, young Mark may have followed them and witnessed Jesus boldly banishing all those who were desecrating this holy place of worship—or he may have later learned what happened from Peter (or from Stephen). Either way, God having already blessed Mark with courage, such an event would no doubt have inspired our young Saint to grow in lion-strength, determined to follow his divine Master's bold example.

Indeed, in light of Mark having met Stephen shortly after this event, given that Stephen was similarly blessed, it is easy to see how Mark and Stephen became the best of friends (together with Mark's older cousin Barnabas, as previously mentioned).

Thus we see the three of them bonded in brotherhood as they rejoicingly accompanied the Blessed Virgin Mary and Mark's mother, and other Holy Women, following their beloved Jesus and His Apostles, listening to their Good Shepherd's wondrous preachings and watching Him perform His many compassionate miracles (all of which probably inspired our lionhearted Saint to write his holy Gospel).

Indeed, not only does Mark's Gospel cover a number of Christ's parables, preachings, and miracles, but it also includes some interesting details not witnessed by Mark but no doubt provided by his fatherly mentor, Peter. For instance, in his first chapter[55] Mark reveals that when Jesus was in the desert forty days and nights and was tempted by Satan, Our Lord "*was with beasts, and the angels ministered to Him*"—prompting us to imagine that this would have been something that Jesus may possibly only have shared with His first chosen Apostles (Peter, Andrew, James and John).

---

[55] Mk. 1:13.

In another instance, Mark's Gospel[56] reveals that when Our Lord was on board a ship with His Apostles on the Sea of Galilee and a great tempest arose threatening to sink their ship, they found Him "*in the hinder part of the ship, sleeping upon a pillow*"—and having awoken their Master, He promptly "*rebuked the wind and said to the sea: Peace, be still. And the wind ceased; and there was made a great calm.*"

Yet another of Peter's valuable sharings is in Mark's description of Christ's Transfiguration, when Jesus appeared to Peter, James and John, shining in all His heavenly glory[57]—that they may believe and never have fear (no doubt this event further inspiring our lionhearted Saint).

Progressing forward in time to when Judas sought to betray Our Lord, we know that Jesus returned to Jerusalem with His Apostles to celebrate His final Paschal dinner. At the time, as previously mentioned, we can imagine Mark's mother and other Holy Women helping the Blessed Virgin Mary to prepare the meal for her Son's Last Supper, while Mark, his cousin and Stephen would have been setting up the dining room with the refectory table and required seating.

Shortly thereafter, although Mark's Gospel[58] conceals his identity, it appears that he was the young man carrying a pitcher of water into the house, whom Jesus had told two of His Apostles to follow that they may know the planned location of the refectory. Later, the evangelist Luke's Gospel[59] reveals that it was actually Peter and John who had followed Mark—no doubt all five friends promptly working together to prepare the table in readiness for the dinner.

Then when Jesus began celebrating His Last Supper with His Twelve Apostles, once again we can picture Mark with his cousin

---

56 Mk. 4:37-39.
57 Mk. 9:1-7.
58 Mk. 14:13-16.
59 Lk. 22:7-10.

Barnabas and their dear friend Stephen in another room, dining with their beloved Virgin Mary, Mark's dear mother and other Holy Women—and would still have been together when Jesus left the house with His Apostles.

Now remembering how the Blessed Virgin Mary had led her loved ones in prayer to the Eternal Father, encouraging them to trust in His holy Will, it appears that at some point during the night our lionhearted Saint had boldly crept out of the house and had fearlessly headed over to the garden of Gethsemani (where he knew Jesus would often take His Apostles to pray). For from his own Gospel,[60] it would seem that Mark was the young man clad only in a loincloth, who was following the cohort that had come to arrest Jesus. His efforts to continue following them were, however, thwarted when one of the soldiers laid hold of him. Promptly releasing his loincloth, our smart young Saint left it in the hands of his captor, thereby enabling his escape. But as he was now left naked, he had to hastily return home under cover of the darkness.

Even so, the next morning Peter would have shared with Mark all that had taken place that night.[61] For after Christ's arrest, we know that Peter had followed the cohort and was in the courtyard close to where Jesus had been taken before the high priest—and albeit from a distance, had helplessly watched his beloved Master being mocked, spat upon and savagely treated. Furthermore, Peter also admitted to Mark that on three occasions (afraid of himself being apprehended) he had denied knowing Jesus; whereupon, after his third denial, he heard a cock crow for the second time in the far distance, reminding him that earlier that same evening his Master had warned that this is what would happen (leaving Peter deeply ashamed as he tearfully fled the scene).[62]

---

[60] Mk. 14:51-52.

[61] Mk. 14:53-65.

[62] Mk. 14:66-72.

Thereafter, Mark's Gospel[63] provides us with a description of Christ's time before Pontius Pilate[64] (who eventually gave in to the chief priests' seditious demands, commanding that Jesus be scourged and then crucified). After they had scourged Our Lord, Mark goes on to describe how His cruel tormenters clothed Him with a purple robe and crowned Him with a ring of thorns; all the while mocking and spitting upon Him—their savage treatment ending after Christ's Crucifixion, Death and Burial.

Mark's final chapter then briefly covers Christ's Resurrection and Ascension, during which time we know that our Saint was with his cousin Barnabas and their dear friend Stephen, witnessing these holy events together as devoted followers of their beloved Risen Lord.

Now ten days after Christ's Ascension, we know that there occurred the miracle of Pentecost—after which event, filled with the fruits of the Holy Ghost, the Apostles began preaching in Jerusalem, and at some point ordained Stephen as one of their seven deacons; followed approximately one year later by Stephen's holy martyrdom. As previously mentioned, we know that the Apostles then sent a number of their disciples away from Jerusalem to avoid the great persecution that had now been unleashed against the Church, although not Mark at this time and apparently not Barnabas (who had left the city to sell all of his inheritance, as later revealed).

On Barnabas' return, the Apostles sent him to Antioch, while Peter took Mark with him to Rome.

Here in Rome, as Latin was the common dialect (different from Aramaic spoken in Peter's Galilean hometown), it is believed that Mark became Peter's interpreter[65]—for having been provided with a sound education, he was able to translate Peter's sermons into Latin

---

63 Mk. 15:2-46.

64 Pontius Pilate, Roman governor of Judea, 26–37 AD.

65 This information confirmed by the famous St. Jerome (c. 340–Sept. 30, 420), ranked first among the ancient exegetes and famed for his extensive knowledge of sacred history.

(which sermons Mark would no doubt have found useful when writing his Gospel).

Indeed, it is here in this city that Mark is said to have completed his evangelical work under the guidance of Peter (believed to have been finalized about ten years after Christ's Ascension); his Gospel being the first-written of the four. Albeit shorter than the other three, it provides a comprehensive outline of Our Lord's divine ministry, and is believed to have set the groundwork for the other evangelists to write their Gospels.

Then at some point while Mark was still with Peter in Rome, they received word that a prophesied famine was about to inflict Judea.[66] So the two of them hastily returned to Jerusalem, where they met up with John[67] and other Apostles who had similarly returned to the city anxious to prepare for the event—to include Mark's cousin Barnabas who had arrived from Antioch (with his co-worker, the apostle Paul). We can imagine Mark and Barnabas (along with the others) rejoicing over their reunion (more than ten years having already passed since they had parted company in Jerusalem).

Sadly, however, on perceiving the Apostles united in his city, King Herod[68] stretched forth his hand to afflict the Church.[69] He first had the Apostle James beheaded with a sword[70]—and seeing that this pleased the Jews, he then had the Prince of Apostles arrested and thrown into a guarded cell (intending to have him killed after the Pasch in a grand public display). Fearing the miraculous powers exercised by the Apostles, the king had Peter placed in chains with a large number of guards surrounding him. But on the last night,

---

[66] Acts 11:28.

[67] Not accompanied by Christ's holy Mother—for he had left her behind in Ephesus.

[68] King Herod Agrippa I, ruled from 41 to 44 AD and died by the Hand of Almighty God (Acts 12:23); grandson of Herod the Great and father of Herod Agrippa II.

[69] Acts 12:1.

[70] Acts 12:2-11.

an angel came to Peter, putting the guards to sleep and breaking the chains that bound him, enabling him to escape. Giving thanks to Almighty God, he hurried to the home of Mark's mother[71] (where all were gathered, earnestly praying for their beloved leader), and oh with what incredulous joy they would have received him. However, to ensure everyone's safety Peter quickly departed from them that same night—and in light of John being the brother of the beheaded James, Peter took his Apostle friend with him.

Now in light of Peter's absence, once it was time for Barnabas to return to Antioch, he offered to take Mark with him. Excited to embark on this new venture, our Saint then left Jerusalem with Barnabas and his co-worker Paul.[72] They were not long in Antioch, however, when the Holy Ghost guided them to take the Word of God to the island of Cyprus.[73]

Here on the island (which happened to be the birthplace of Barnabas), Mark witnessed both his cousin's gentle way of encouraging souls to convert, and Paul's equal success through his zealous preaching—promptly inspiring our lionhearted Saint to preach Christ's gospel message wherever his fatherly mentor would send him. So after the three of them had completed their missionary work on the island, Mark left Barnabas and Paul to return to Jerusalem[74] (by which time Peter had already returned to the city).

Upon perceiving his adopted son's eagerness to preach the Word of God, Peter sent Mark to Alexandria in the land of Egypt—where, filled with lionhearted enthusiasm, our Saint converted many souls. In fact he was so successful that he was even able to have a first Christian church built in this city, in spite of being faced with strong opposition from the Romans.

---

[71] Acts 12:12.
[72] Acts 12:25.
[73] Acts 13:4.
[74] Acts 13:13.

Indeed, there is a legend that when the jealous Romans threw Mark into a den of lions, the beasts refused to attack or eat him. Instead, in clear recognition of his strength (and no doubt drawn to his gentle Christ-like love) they calmly laid at his feet while he tenderly caressed them. His captors then promptly released our Saint, fearful over what they beheld.

Thereafter, Mark left to preach to the Anchorites, a large group of hermits living in the Egyptian desert who had not heard of Christianity. In his lionhearted way, Mark was similarly able to convert a vast number of them—thereafter becoming known as the "*Father of the Anchorites.*"

Then when Mark learned that Peter had returned to Jerusalem to establish a council to debate the issue of circumcision,[75] he left Egypt and headed over to the city, where he joyfully met up with his fatherly mentor, along with Barnabas and Paul (both of whom had arrived from Antioch where they were once again preaching at the time).

Now after the decree was finalized and Barnabas and Paul returned to Antioch to convey the results to the converted Gentiles, in due time Barnabas returned to Jerusalem hoping to take Mark with him back to his birthplace to see how the faithful were doing in Cyprus. So with Peter's blessing, the two of them returned to the island.[76]

With much rejoicing the brethren received their beloved Barnabas and his much loved Mark, such that the two of them remained preaching together for a good ten years, right up until Barnabas' holy martyrdom (described in the following chapter). Even thereafter, determined to continue his dear cousin's good work, our lionhearted Saint boldly preached on the island for a further three

[75] Covered in more detail in the following chapter.

[76] Acts 15:39.

years—until he learned that Peter had returned to Rome, whereupon he left Cyprus to spend some time with him.

In Rome, however, during their time together, Emperor Nero began persecuting the Christians. So it appears that Peter ordered Mark to leave the city—for Tradition dictates that during this time, our Saint returned to Alexandria.

On his arrival back in this city, Mark happily discovered that the Christian converts had grown in number. So he promptly set up the first Christian school in close proximity to the church that he had previously established in this major Egyptian city—which school is believed to have become the fruitful mother of many illustrious doctors and bishops.

Yet in spite of Mark's successful efforts, there remained those devoted to their pagan gods. Indeed, while celebrating the Feast of Christ's Resurrection in the year 68 AD, as this day coincided with a pagan celebration for the Egyptian god named Syrabis, a large number of pagans assembled and forced their way into the church where our fifty-six year old Saint was preaching to the Christians on this holy Feast Day of Our Lord.

They seized hold of Mark, bound him with a thick rope and dragged him through the stony streets with such severity that his flesh was torn and the ground covered in his blood. They then cast him into a dark prison cell where divine revelation reveals that an angel of the Lord appeared to our lionhearted Saint, telling him:

"*O Mark, the good servant, rejoice for your name has been written in the book of life, and you have been counted among the congregation of the saints.*"

The angel then disappeared and Jesus appeared to His saintly Mark, giving him further comfort and strength.

The following morning, the pagans came and repeated their torturous treatment of our beloved Saint, whereupon that night he died of his fatal injuries in his prison cell.

Historical records determine that Mark was then buried under the church that he had founded in Alexandria. However, in 828 AD his remains are believed to have been stolen by merchants and taken to Venice—where they remain to this day in a church dedicated to our Saint, named St. Mark's Basilica.

In light of St. Mark's lionhearted love of Jesus influencing his life since his teenage years, it is hardly surprising that Our Lord sent an angel to comfort him during his last hours, revealing to him his heavenly reward—further confirmed when Jesus Himself then appeared to His beloved faithful disciple.

May the story of our saintly Mark's life and ministry inspire us to boldly soldier on through the battles of life with a lion-determination to keep the Faith as taught by Jesus and handed down through His Apostles—so that some day we too may have our name written in the book of life.

Saint Barnabas
(1 AD—61 AD)

CHAPTER 3

Saint Barnabas

June 11

Saint Barnabas, like his young cousin Mark and their good friend Stephen, was also blessed with saintly courage; his bold preaching that Jesus is Christ the Messiah ultimately earning him a holy martyrdom at the hands of the non-believing, envious Jews—his death believed to have occurred in 61 AD.

Born to wealthy parents of the tribe of Levi in the ancient city of Salamis[77] in Cyprus in the year 1 AD, from the Acts of the Apostles[78] we learn that although our Saint's parents had named him Joseph at birth, the Apostles renamed him Barnabas, meaning "*Son of Consolation.*" For once they got to know him, they quickly perceived that our Saint was blessed with a most kind and compassionate heart, seeking to console and comfort whenever the need arose.

Now while Tradition dictates that Barnabas was schooled in Jerusalem, at the time of Mark's mother purchasing that large house, he had already returned to his hometown (his schooling having just ended). However, in light of his filial connection with Mark, after the death of both his parents Barnabas returned to Jerusalem to reside with Mark and his mother—which is how he came to know the

---

[77] Later renamed Constantia in the fourth century.

[78] Acts 4:36.

Apostles and Stephen, and of course, to love Jesus and His Blessed Mother.

Hence we see Barnabas with his cousin Mark and their dear friend Stephen accompanying the Blessed Virgin Mary and Mark's mother and other Holy Women, as they followed Jesus and His Apostles whenever possible—listening and learning from Christ's wondrous preachings, and marveling over His many miracles. On those occasions when Barnabas would be alone with Mark and Stephen, in light of him being the eldest we can imagine him leading their many discussions over what they had learned; the three of them growing in holiness as devout Early Christians bonded in brotherhood.

And as previously mentioned, we know that they remained united in their friendship throughout the events that followed their beloved Master's Crucifixion, to include the time of Christ's Resurrection—first heralded by Mary Magdalen claiming to have seen Jesus. Even as the day progressed without any sign of their Risen Master, given that Barnabas was blessed with a particularly kind and consoling heart, we can readily envisage him endeavoring to comfort all those who were feeling somewhat disheartened and filled with doubt—when unexpectedly, in the late afternoon of that same day, we know that two disciples arrived at the house similarly claiming to have seen Jesus.[79] Expounding upon their story, they were traveling along the highway to a town called Emmaus, they said, when about sixty furlongs from Jerusalem they were joined by a Stranger who asked why they were troubled. Somewhat surprised that the man appeared not to have heard all that had happened recently in Jerusalem, the disciples explained that their Messiah, Jesus of Nazareth, "*mighty in work and word before God and all the people,*" had been unjustly condemned and crucified just three days previously—adding sadly that they had hoped that He would be the one who would

[79] Lk. 24:13-33.

redeem Israel. They then went on to inform the Stranger that some women from their own company early that very morning had gone to the tomb and found the great stone rolled back, and the body of their Messiah no longer within. Furthermore, the women claimed to have seen a vision of angels, who told them that Jesus is alive—causing much alarm and confusion.

Much to the disciples' amazement, the Stranger (who they did not recognize as one of their own) responded that surely Jesus was to have suffered these things before entering into His glory—as the prophets had so foretold. And He went on to provide a complete history going back to the time of Moses and all that had been said about the Messiah. Their hearts already burning within them, on approaching the town of Emmaus, the disciples invited the Stranger to dine with them. As they sat together at table, the Stranger took bread, blessed, and broke it—whereupon the disciples promptly recognized the Stranger as their beloved Jesus! However, as they both stared at their Master with incredulous joy, He vanished from their sight.

Yet in spite of the disciples' sharing, most of the household still greeted the news with doubt (although not Barnabas, Mark and Stephen, as previously mentioned)—when we know that Jesus suddenly appeared in all His Risen glory, inviting all those who did not believe to feel His hands and His feet bearing the deep imprint where the nails had transfixed Him to the Cross. He even ate a piece of broiled fish and a honeycomb,[80] that all may believe that He was no ghost but had truly risen from the dead as he had said He would; everyone now filled with indescribable joy.

Forty days later when it was time for their Risen Lord to ascend into Heaven, we can once again visualize our Saint with Mark and Stephen accompanying their beloved Virgin Mary and Mark's dear

---

[80] Lk. 24:40-42.

mother, along with other Holy Women, as they followed the Apostles up Mount Olivet to meet their Risen Christ for the last time.

After Christ's Ascension, as they descended the mountain that day, no doubt our saintly Barnabas in his typically consoling way, would have reminded Mark and Stephen that Peter had previously told them that during their Master's Last Supper, Jesus had explained to His Apostles that He would be leaving them to return to His Father in Heaven and at the time had gently comforted them by adding:[81]

"*If you loved Me, you would indeed be glad, because I go to the Father.*"

Going further, our Saint would also have reminded Mark and Stephen that Jesus had promised that He would be sending the Holy Ghost, the Paraclete, who would gift the Apostles with a complete understanding of all that He was saying.

And sure enough, when the miracle of Pentecost occurred, we know that their Apostle friends were indeed blessed with these gifts, enabling them to preach on the wondrous importance of knowing, loving and serving the Triune Godhead (Father, Son and Holy Ghost) leading all faithful souls into the glorified joy of God's heavenly Kingdom.[82]

Now in light of Barnabas having experienced the mighty wind that resounded throughout the whole house of Mark's mother on the day of Pentecost, we see that he felt inspired to return to his hometown and sell all of his inheritance,[83] promptly returning to Jerusalem where he "*laid it at the feet of the Apostles.*" On perceiving their disciple's virtuous benevolence, it was at this time that the Apostles sent our dear Barnabas to Antioch[84] (it being an import-

---

[81] Jn. 14:26-28.
[82] I Pet. 1:7-8.
[83] Acts 4:37.
[84] Acts 11:22-23.

ant city in the Roman Empire[85])—clearly confident that our Saint would be most successful.

And true to their inspired confidence, in light of Barnabas being "*a good man, full of the Holy Ghost and of faith,*"[86] throughout his ten years (and more) of preaching in this city—his gentle way of encouraging souls to convert resulted in an abundance of success. So much so, that in due time as the number of converts continued to increase he needed help to preach to them all. So knowing as he did that the Apostles had sent Paul to his hometown of Tarsus, our Saint sped over there in search of his friend (whom he had previously met in Jerusalem some three years after Stephen's holy martyrdom). And having tracked him down, the two of them traveled back to Antioch[87]—where they worked well together, preaching to the vast numbers.

Then just one year later, they received news of the prophesied famine that was about to inflict the whole of Judea. So the two of them gathered supplies for their Christian brethren and hastened back to Jerusalem (where, as previously mentioned, Barnabas was excited to reconnect with his young cousin Mark after their many years of not seeing each other).

Now during their time in this holy city, we know that King Herod beheaded the Apostle James with a sword and then imprisoned Peter, being Prince of the Apostles. And after Peter's escape (thanks to divine intervention), Barnabas returned to Antioch with Paul, this time taking his dear cousin with them—where we know the three of them remained until the Holy Ghost called them to head over to Cyprus to spread Christ's gospel message throughout the island.

---

85 Principal city in Ancient Syria and fourth largest city of the Roman Empire (after Rome, Ephesus and Alexandria), becoming at that time an important center of early Christianity.

86 Acts 11:24.

87 Acts 11:25.

Expounding upon their ministry work, as Cyprus was the place of Barnabas' birth, our Saint would naturally have felt a close connection with the people in the land of his birth—and in his gentle way of encouraging, once again converted many souls; his success enhanced by his good friend Paul and his lionhearted cousin Mark. In fact we note that by the time of their arrival in Paphos, their reputation had spread across the island, such that the proconsul of Cyprus, Sergius Paulus, called upon them as he wanted to hear the Word of God.[88]

As they began preaching to him, suddenly a Jewish magician (a false prophet) named Elymas approached, and withstood them—whereupon Paul boldly told the man:

"*O full of all guile, and of all deceit, child of the devil, enemy of all justice, thou ceasest not to pervert the right ways of the Lord. And now behold, the hand of the Lord is upon thee, and thou shalt be blind, not seeing the sun for a time.*"

And much to the amazement of Sergius Paulus, there fell upon the magician a dark mist, leaving him in a state of blindness—promptly drawing the proconsul to believe in the power of Almighty God and in the sacred teachings of His Divine Son, as witnessed by the three disciples standing before him.

After establishing more Christian communities and Christ's Early Church on the island, we remember that Barnabas and Paul then returned to Antioch—while their lionhearted Mark returned to Jerusalem.

Progressing with Barnabas and Paul's arrival back in Antioch, once again we see that their preaching continued to enthrall the Gentiles, converting many throughout the city;[89] so much so that certain Jews, seeing the great multitudes, were envious of their pop-

[88] Acts 13:6-12.
[89] Acts 13:43-44.

ularity and accused them of blasphemy, whereupon Barnabas and Paul boldly told them:[90]

"*To you it behoved us first to speak the Word of God: but because you reject it, and judge yourselves unworthy of Eternal Life, behold we turn to the Gentiles. For so the Lord hath commanded us: I have set thee to be the light of the Gentiles; that thou mayest be for salvation unto the utmost part of the earth.*"

While the Gentiles rejoiced and were glad, the Jews went forth and stirred up the people, raising persecution against our Saint and his dear friend Paul[91]—and having succeeded in banishing them from the region, Barnabas and Paul then traveled to Iconium. Here in this ancient capital city they were successful for the most part in converting many of the Gentiles, and indeed some of the Jews, although there still remained a number of Jews who refused to accept that Jesus was Christ the Messiah, and in their typically envious way, stirred up confusion and division among the people.[92] Yet undeterred, our gentle-hearted Barnabas reached out to comfort and console the Christian brethren, backed by the stalwart efforts of his good friend Paul, such that they were able to continue preaching for quite some time—until the unbelievers plotted to have them stoned.[93]

So the two of them fled to the nearby ancient district of Lycaonia (now modern-day Turkey), where they first traveled to Lystra to preach Christ's gospel message. They were not here long, however, for after Paul cured a cripple who was unable to walk, the people declared that "*the gods are come down upon us in the likeness of men.*"[94] Even as Barnabas and Paul cried out to the people telling them that they were mere mortals like the rest of them, the people were not

---

[90] Acts 13:45-47.
[91] Acts 13:50-51.
[92] Acts 14:1-4.
[93] Acts 14:5.
[94] Acts 14:6-17.

convinced and wanted to make sacrifices to them. Furthermore, in the midst of all this turmoil, there came to Lystra certain of the non-believing Jews who had banished them from Antioch and Iconium—now stirring the people to violence against them and driving them out of the city. And having perceived Paul as the chief speaker, they even hurled stones at him, seeking to stone him to death.[95]

But he miraculously survived, and Barnabas took his injured friend to Derbe near by,[96] where he looked after him (no doubt in his gifted way, gently encouraging his dear Paul to not give up hope). Indeed, so successful were Barnabas' saintly efforts that once recovered and his strength restored, Paul boldly suggested that the two of them return to all three cities from where they had been brutally banished, for he now felt encouraged to go forth and exhort the brethren to remain strong in the Faith, even in the face of opposition and persecution.

So they first traveled back to Lystra[97]—whereupon during this visit, the disciple Timothy, a teenager at the time, upon hearing Barnabas and Paul preaching, promptly converted (in due time becoming another Early Martyr who died in the First Century—as revealed in the following chapter).

Now unlike the previous occasion when Barnabas and Paul were in this city, during this visit they were actually faced with no opposition; such that their stalwart efforts met with much success. In fact, on returning to Iconium and Antioch (as planned) they similarly met with no opposition, enabling them to ordain priests in all three cities.[98]

Feeling greatly encouraged, the two of them then passed through the region of Pisidia and returned to the country of Pamphylia,[99]

---

95 Acts 14:18.
96 Acts 14:19.
97 Acts 14:20.
98 Acts 14:22.
99 Acts 14:23-24.

where they preached Christ's gospel message in its capital city of Perge, before continuing on to the city of Attalia, located on the Mediterranean coast. Here they felt prompted to once again return to Antioch.

So our Saint and his dear friend boarded a ship and set sail for their favorite city, where they remained for a good length of time until they came up against some who had come from Judea and were claiming that unless the people were circumcised after the manner of Moses, they would not be saved;[100] whereupon they then traveled back to Jerusalem to hear what the Apostles had to say.

On their arrival, as Mark had returned from Egypt, we can imagine the three of them rejoicing over their being able to spend time together. Then when the Apostles established a council to discuss the matter with the ancients, we note that after some debate,[101] Peter as Prince of the Apostles stood forth and spoke at some length, outlining the history of Moses and ending with the words:

"*Now therefore, why tempt your God to put a yoke upon the necks of the disciples, which neither our fathers nor we have been able to bear?*"

Backed by his good friend Paul, Barnabas then stood forth and in his usual way of consoling in times of confusion, shared with the council the great signs and wonders that God had wrought among the Gentiles whom they had converted.[102] So after some further discussion, it was finally decreed that this Mosaic law need not be applied to the converted Gentiles.[103]

Now while Mark remained with Peter in Jerusalem, we know that Barnabas and Paul left to return to Antioch[104] (to impart the decree of the council)—this time taking with them two well respected disciples (Silas and Judas Barsabas). After the four of them had

---

100 Acts 15:1-2.
101 Acts 15:7-10.
102 Acts 15:12.
103 Acts 15:13-24.
104 Acts 15:25-27.

imparted the good news to the Gentile converts in and around the city, Judas Barsabas returned to Jerusalem[105] while Silas remained with our Saint and Paul.

Then once it was time for the three of them to move on, Paul proposed that they revisit the brethren in all of the cities where they had already preached—whereupon Barnabas suggested that perhaps they could also take his cousin Mark along with them.[106] However, in light of Mark having left them previously, Paul was not keen on the idea—so it was at this point that Barnabas left Paul and Silas, hoping to track down his cousin in Jerusalem.

On his arrival back home, our Saint found his dear cousin (who was still with Peter at the time)—and with Peter's blessing, he and Mark then left the city to return to Cyprus to check on how the faithful were doing.

After their arrival, we know that they remained in Cyprus for a good ten years, expanding the Early Church right across the island—Barnabas' gentle way of consoling and converting blending well with the lionhearted spirit of his young Mark.

However, in spite of their successful efforts, there still remained certain non-believing Jews who stubbornly refused to convert, and were filled with envy as they watched the number of Christians increasing on a regular basis.

Then one day, in the year 61 AD, Tradition dictates that while our sixty-year old Barnabas was preaching in the synagogue in Salamis, certain of these Jews, enraged by our Saint's preaching, dragged him forth from out of the synagogue and after the most inhuman of tortures, stoned him to death—just as Mark arrived on the scene.

Devastated over the death of his beloved Barnabas and determined to protect his remains, Mark had the body of his dear cousin privately interred in this city of Barnabas' birth (placing over his

[105] Acts 15:34-35.
[106] Acts 15:36-38.

chest, a handwritten copy of the Apostle Matthew's Gospel which our saintly Barnabas happened to have been using during his sermon that day).

While the location of Barnabas' burial was not known for many centuries, it is believed to have been revealed by Barnabas himself when he appeared in a dream to Archbishop Anthemius[107] of Cyprus around 480 AD—whereupon his remains were promptly discovered the very next day, buried in an old tomb under a carob tree in Salamis still with the handwritten Gospel intact. As this greatly impressed the Emperor Zeno,[108] he promptly financed the construction of a basilica near the site of our Saint's tomb. Then in the seventeenth century, after the basilica was badly damaged during Arab raids, a monastery was built in honor of our beloved Barnabas close to the ruins—currently housing his tomb in one of its chapels.

Saint Barnabas, renowned for his gentle, charitable way of consoling and comforting in times of turmoil and confusion, quickly became known after his death as the Patron Saint of Peacemaking.

As we contemplate Barnabas' saintly virtues that set him on the path of holiness as a "*Son of Consolation,*" may we too feel inspired to treat our fellowman with that same Christ-like consoling, encouraging spirit.

---

107 Anthemius of Constantia, Archbishop of Cyprus in the late fifth century.

108 Emperor Zeno (425–April 9, 491); Eastern Roman emperor from 474 to 475 and again from 476 to 491 during a time of domestic revolts and religious dissension, which plagued his reign.

Saint Timothy
(17 AD—97 AD)

CHAPTER 4

Saint Timothy

January 24

Saint Timothy, who became known for his soft-spoken, gentle way, like Barnabas was also blessed with a uniquely consoling and compassionate heart—his loving concern (as a Bishop) to protect his flock against paganism ultimately earning him a holy martyrdom (believed to have occurred in 97 AD).

Historical records reveal that our Saint was born in 17 AD to a Greek Gentile father and a Jewish mother in the ancient city of Lystra—which city at the time of Timothy's birth was still beholden to its pagan origins, having never been introduced to Christianity. However, as previously mentioned we know that Timothy was a teenager (at the time in his late teens) when Barnabas and Paul brought the Word of God to his hometown. After accompanying his Jewish mother Eunice and his Jewish grandmother Lois into the local synagogue to hear the disciples preach, young Timothy and his mother and grandmother all converted to the Faith (thereby enabling our Saint to grow up in a most devout household, for both his mother and grandmother became known for their piety).[109] In fact, from the time of his conversion, Timothy eagerly sought to learn more about Christ, becoming a most learned Early Christian

[109] II Tim. 1:5.

over time[110] (living up to his Greek name, meaning "*one who honors God*").

Some thirteen years when Paul returned to Lystra,[111] this time with his co-worker Silas (Barnabas having already left Paul to take his cousin Mark with him back to Cyprus), Timothy had grown into a young man and was already held in high regard among the Christian brethren, both in his hometown and in the neighboring city of Iconium.[112]

So once Paul was personally introduced to Timothy, upon sensing a holiness in our Saint, he invited him to accompany both himself and Silas on their next missionary journey. Already feeling inspired, Timothy promptly rose to the challenge, whereupon Paul became his spiritual father (and at some point ordained him to the priesthood[113]). Moreover, knowing that Timothy's father was a Gentile, in spite of the recent decree by the Jerusalem council (determining that converted Gentiles need not be circumcised), in his fatherly concern to protect his priestly brother against any negative reaction from the Jews, Paul had Timothy circumcised.[114]

Thus prepared, our Saint joyfully joined Paul and Silas, leaving family and country to embark upon this next leg of his spiritual journey; the three of them quickly becoming the best of friends, united in their love of Christ and in their holy cause.

After leaving Lystra, they first traveled through the neighboring cities delivering the council's decree; at the same time confirming the brethren[115]—the numbers increasing daily (Paul no doubt quietly enjoying the success of his priestly brother Timothy, whose gentle way of preaching helped to convert many souls).

---

110 II Tim. 3:15.
111 Acts 16:1.
112 Acts 16:2.
113 I Tim. 4:14.
114 Acts 16:3.
115 Acts 16:4-5.

In due time, as they progressed through the mountainous region of Phrygia and the neighboring country of Galatia, the Holy Ghost forbade them to preach Christ's gospel message in Asia at this time,[116] and even as they passed through Mysia, a region in the northwest of Asia, intending to proceed to Bythynia along its northern edge, the spirit of Jesus suffered them not to progress.[117] So Timothy, Paul, and Silas left Mysia and headed for the ancient city of Troas on the coast—where they met up with the evangelist Luke (who quickly sought to join them in their apostolic crusade).

Indeed, we note from the Acts of the Apostles (where Luke uses the pronoun "we") that the four of them stayed together in this city—until Paul had a vision at night of a man seeking their help in Macedonia; whereupon Timothy, Paul and Silas left Troas with their new co-worker and friend, and headed over to Philippi, it being a major city in this Roman province.[118]

Upon their arrival, Luke tells us[119] that the Holy Ghost directed them to an outdoor prayer group on the Sabbath, where they met a woman named Lydia. After listening to Paul's preaching, she not only asked to be baptized (along with her household) but she invited all four of them to stay in her home until it was time for them to move on.

However, they were not long here in Philippi for after Paul healed a girl possessed with a demonic spirit, this caused an uproar among certain of the Roman citizens, resulting in Paul and Silas being beaten with rods and cast into prison.[120] Upon learning what had happened to their dear friends, Timothy and Luke invited all of Lydia's household to join them in prayer—encouraging them to place their trust in the power of Almighty God. And indeed, in the

---

[116] Acts 16:6.
[117] Acts 16:7.
[118] Acts 16:9-12.
[119] Acts 16:13-15.
[120] Acts 16:23-24.

aftermath of their prayers, they later learned that at the stroke of midnight, while Paul and Silas were praying out loud in their prison cell, an earthquake suddenly shook the building.[121] The force broke their chains, and the door of their cell flew open. Their prison keeper awoke, and in the dull lighting in the corridor, upon seeing the door of his prisoners' cell standing wide open, believed that they had escaped—and terrified of his punishment, he drew forth his sword to end his own life.[122] But as Paul could see him in the dim lighting, he cried out to him from the darkness of their cell (determined to prove the power of Almighty God) telling him not to harm himself, for they were still here. Grabbing a light, the keeper ran down the corridor and finding his prisoners with their chains fallen away—and remembering how they were praying out loud to their Lord God—now fell on his knees before them, asking how he could be saved. And after listening to Paul, he promptly converted.[123] He even took them to his home that night, where his family tended to their wounds and gave them dinner, and as Paul and Silas preached the Word of God to them, they each and all similarly believed and were baptized.

Now the following morning, upon hearing what happened, the magistrates (not wishing the story to be spread around) ordered Paul and Silas to leave Philippi right away.[124] So the two of them hurried to the home of Lydia—the whole household rejoicing over their dear friends' release. And on hearing about the earthquake, it appears that Timothy and Luke's faith in the power of Almighty God was further strengthened—as seen in Luke's bold determination to continue preaching in this city in spite of this recent event, and Timothy's stalwart resolve to press on with Paul and Silas, even knowing they would be facing many more such challenges in the years ahead.

---

121 Acts 16:25-26.
122 Acts 16:27-28.
123 Acts 16:30-34.
124 Acts 16:26.

So after leaving Philippi, Timothy traveled with Paul and Silas passing through the nearby cities of Amphipolis and Apollonia in Macedonia to arrive in the seaport of Thessalonica.[125] Here in this capital city, they went into the local synagogue and courageously reasoned with the Jews that it behoved Christ to suffer and rise again from the dead.[126] However, while their preaching met with some success (especially among the Gentiles who attended at the synagogue and warmly greeted all three of them), a number of the unconverted Jews, in their typical way, were moved with envy. They grouped together those of like mind, and stirred up the people, setting the city in an uproar.[127] So the Christian brethren, fearing for their disciples' lives, dispatched all three of them under cover of darkness to the Macedonian city of Berea close by, where the Jews were more open to Christ's gospel message.[128]

Alas, not long after they arrived in Berea, the envy-driven Jews in Thessalonica traveled to this small city and once again stirred up the people.[129] So the Christian brethren, fearing for Paul's life (he being the main speaker) promptly sent him away by ship, while Timothy and Silas boldly remained in the city for quite some time.[130] For in his soft-spoken, gentle way, Timothy was able to calm the rioters, preaching Christ's peace to them and successfully dampening their hostility.

Then when Paul finally arrived in Athens (having been taken there by his rescuers),[131] he sent urgent word to our Saint and Silas calling on them to leave Berea right away and come to him—whereupon the two of them promptly departed and headed over to the city. In the meantime, while Paul awaited their arrival, his spirit was

[125] Acts 17:1.
[126] Acts 17:2-3.
[127] Acts 17:4-5.
[128] Acts 17:10-11.
[129] Acts 17:13.
[130] Acts 17:14.
[131] Acts 17:15.

aroused as he perceived the whole of Athens was given to idolatry.[132] Paul went into the synagogue and disputed with the Jews, and even preached in the marketplace the importance of knowing and serving Jesus Christ. However, while some believed, there were still others who mocked the Word of God.[133] In fact, during this time Paul received word that their Thessalonian brethren had come under severe persecution by like-minded, non-believing Jews. So upon Timothy and Silas' arrival in Athens, Paul promptly sent them back to Thessalonica, knowing he could trust in their ability to comfort and strengthen the brethren[134] (while he himself departed from Athens and went to Corinth[135] in the neighboring province of Achaia).

After our Saint, with Silas at his side, had successfully reassured the Thessalonian brethren to remain strong in the Faith even when faced with opposition and persecution,[136] they then traveled south of Macedonia[137] to meet up with Paul in Corinth—where they found him earnestly preaching in the synagogue on the Sabbath, testifying that Jesus is Christ the Messiah.

Sadly, yet again history repeated itself as a number of the Jews still refused to convert; their blasphemous attitude no doubt prompting Timothy to suggest to Paul that they reach out to the Gentiles instead[138]—as they did in Thessalonica. And sure enough, many of the Greek Gentiles here in Corinth then believed and were baptized.[139]

To further encourage His priestly disciples, Jesus then appeared to Paul in a night vision, telling him:[140]

---

132 Acts 17:16-17.
133 Acts 17:32.
134 I Thess. 3:2.
135 Acts 18:1.
136 I Thess. 3:6-7.
137 Acts 18:5.
138 Acts 18:6.
139 Acts 18:8.
140 Acts 18:9-10.

"Do not fear, but speak; and hold not thy peace, because I am with thee: and no man shall set upon thee, to hurt thee for I have much people in this city."

So they remained in the city for a year and six months continuing to preach the Word of God.[141]

Thereafter, while Timothy and Paul left Corinth, the Scriptures provide no further information as to what happened to their co-worker Silas (who may have remained in Corinth for a time or he may have gone to Rome, in light of the Apostle Peter referring to him as a *"faithful brother"* of the Early Church[142]). However, as his name is not included in the Roman Martyrology of Saints, we are drawn to believe that once it was time for dear Silas to depart from the challenges of this life, he must have died a natural death.

Turning now to Timothy and Paul's departure from Corinth, the two of them traveled to Ephesus; at first for just a short visit; followed later by a longer one. Indeed, this second visit lasted a good two years,[143] during which time we can imagine both of them preaching, converting and baptizing, as they worked together expanding the Early Church—our Saint continuing to rejoice as God wrought many miracles by the hand of his much loved and respected Paul.[144]

Pausing for a moment, we know that Ephesus became home to the Blessed Virgin Mary, for after Jesus while dying on the Cross had given His Mother into the care of His favorite Apostle,[145] once John decided to make Ephesus his homebase, Tradition dictates that he had a safe haven built for his beloved Virgin Mary on the outskirts of the city.[146] However, it would seem that Timothy may never have

---

141 Acts 18:11.
142 I Pet. 5:12.
143 Acts 18:19-21; 19:10.
144 Acts 19:11.
145 Jn. 19:27.
146 This home of the Blessed Virgin Mary (commonly referred to as "Mother Mary's House"), after her death became a Catholic shrine, and even to this

met Christ's Blessed Mother for before his first visit to Ephesus, the holy Virgin had already left the city to return to Jerusalem—that she may die in the same room where her precious Son had celebrated His Last Supper (which room later became known as the Cenacle) surrounded by her dearly loved Apostles and the Holy Women who had remained her very dear friends.[147]

Even so, our Saint would of course have known all about the Blessed Virgin Mary, and as a devout Early Christian would have loved and respected her as the Mother of our Redeemer.

Now after their two years in Ephesus, Paul sent his dear Timothy back to Macedonia[148] (this time with another disciple named Erastus)—agreeing that he would later meet up with Timothy in Philippi. Here in Macedonia, it appears that our Saint connected with a number of other disciples,[149] no doubt each of them, like Erastus, learning from Timothy's gentle way of preaching Christ's gospel message and exhorting the brethren to remain strong in the Faith.

In due time, our Saint then traveled back to Philippi as agreed, where he not only met up with Paul, but also their dear friend Luke.[150] For indeed, Luke had remained in Philippi for a further six years after Timothy and Paul had left the city. Rejoicing together over their reunion, the three of them then left Philippi, once again united in their holy cause—and sailed back to Troas where they abode for seven days preaching and exhorting the brethren in their usual way.

---

day remains a popular pilgrimage site.

147 Tradition not only confirms the above, but further reveals that after her death, the Blessed Virgin Mary was buried east of the city in the Valley of Cedron (also known as the Valley of Josaphat) at the foot of Mount Olives—where three days later the Apostle Thomas witnessed her being Assumed into Heaven.

148 Acts 19:22.

149 Acts 20:4.

150 Acts 20:6.

During their time in this ancient city, Luke tells us that on the Lord's day when they and the faithful had assembled in a large upper chamber to break bread,[151] in light of knowing that they would be leaving the next day, Paul discoursed with the faithful late into the night. Close to midnight, a young man named Eutychus who was sitting on an inside window ledge, dropped off to sleep—falling out of the open window to his death. However, Paul went to him and through another wondrous miracle brought the man back to life (no doubt continuing to leave both Timothy and Luke overawed by the God-given gift with which their dearly loved apostle had been blessed).

The next morning, Paul opted to leave Timothy and Luke to sail around the small peninsula to Assos on their own, while he traveled overland, agreeing to meet up with them in the seaport once they had landed[152] (the plan being for the three of them thereafter to continue by sea to Ephesus). Given that his beloved Timothy suffered from an unpleasant and painful abdominal health issue,[153] we are drawn to imagine that possibly Paul deliberately left the two of them to travel this short journey from Troas to Assos in the hope that Luke (who was a doctor before his priestly vocation) would be able to provide Timothy with some helpful medical advice. Indeed, once the three of them were back together and had set sail for Ephesus, it would seem that during their journey Luke may have suggested to Paul that Timothy should curtail his missionary travels to lessen the bad effect on his stomach. For in due time we note that once they had landed in Ephesus, after preaching together in this city for three years,[154] Paul made the decision to leave his *"beloved son in faith"*[155]

---

151 Acts 20:7-10.
152 Acts 20:13.
153 Our beloved Timothy later becoming known as the Patron Saint of Stomach Ailments.
154 Acts 20:31.
155 I Tim. 1:2-3.

here in Ephesus, as he and Luke would be taking a lengthy sea voyage through the various seaports of the Mediterranean in order to arrive in Jerusalem in time to commemorate the day of Pentecost.

Furthermore, in light of Paul having already noted the high regard with which the brethren upheld his beloved Timothy, he ordained our Saint as their first Bishop of Ephesus (confirming the tremendous respect that he himself had for his soft-spoken, valiant son in faith with whom we know he had traveled and preached for a good number of years).

Thereafter, having called together all the ancients of the Church, Paul preached to them for the last time, expounding upon the role of a bishop, and exhorting them to remain strong in the Faith as he had done over the many years of his trials and persecutions.[156] In fact as Paul had further told them that he suspected "*bands and afflictions*" awaited him in Jerusalem, we can readily picture our saintly Timothy (mindful of when he and Luke had invited Lydia's household to pray with them during Paul and Silas' imprisonment in Philippi) now playing a major role as their first Bishop in assembling the large group of faithful that all may kneel down on the seashore and pray for their much respected apostle, before Paul and Luke boarded their ship bound for the holy city.[157]

Now in light of Timothy's long time association with his beloved Paul and his close friendship with his dear Luke, we can imagine their parting not at all an easy one. However, they remained in contact, and in due time once Paul and Luke ended up in Rome (where Paul was being held under house arrest with a soldier keeping him under guard while he awaited judgment[158]), he sent a letter to his dear Timothy[159] asking him to come to Rome with all haste, "*for I*

[156] Acts 20:17-30.
[157] Acts 20:36.
[158] Acts 28:16.
[159] II Tim. 4:6.

am now even ready to be sacrificed: and the time of my dissolution is at hand."

Once united, the three of them would have greatly rejoiced over their time together, perhaps Timothy staying in the large house where Paul was being held as a prisoner and where Luke may also have been residing—leaving us to speculate that albeit Paul was barred from leaving the house, possibly Timothy and Luke were at liberty to go forth and preach in the city, confirming the faithful here in Rome where Peter, Prince of the Apostles, had already established the Early Church.

The three of them were not long together, however, when the Jews surprised Paul by deciding to release him. So Paul then left Rome for a while, as did Luke, and of course our Timothy returned to Ephesus.

Upon our Saint's arrival in Ephesus, we can imagine the brethren joyfully greeting their much loved and respected Bishop, for they would have missed their gentle shepherd who, in his typical Christ-like way, looked after his flock with tender, loving care; at the same time overseeing his diocesan priests as their friend, brother and spiritual father—for such was the nature of our saintly Timothy.

For some fifteen years after his return to Ephesus, our Saint continued to tender his flock as their beloved Bishop before it was time for him to depart from this life. On this very sad day for all of his devoted brethren, Tradition dictates that our Saint suffered a terrible martyrdom. For, as an eighty-year old Bishop, when he tried to stop a pagan procession in his city, the enraged mob had our Timothy viciously beaten, dragged through the streets, and then cruelly stoned to death.

Thereafter, while our dear Saint was buried in Ephesus, come the fourth century his relics were transferred to Constantinople and placed in the Church of the Holy Apostles near the tomb of his close friend Luke and that of the Apostle Andrew. Then in the thirteenth century, in the year 1239, his remains were transferred to a crypt in the Cathedral of Saint Mary of the Purification in the town of Termoli in central Italy (placed under a marble tombstone bearing an inscription: "*In the year of the Lord 1239. Here rests in peace the body of the blessed Timothy, disciple of the blessed apostle Paul.*"); this Cathedral later survived first an earthquake in 1464, and then an attack by the Ottoman Turks in 1566. Yet after restoration works were undertaken to the Cathedral on both occasions, our Saint's relics, enshrined under his marble tombstone, were each time successfully retrieved—the Blessed Virgin Mary (as Saint Mary of the Purification) seen to be protecting the body of her Divine Son's gentle, beloved servant, that he may never be forgotten.

In reviewing the life of dear Saint Timothy, we see that there is much we can learn from him, for he set an example of consistent faith from a very young age, mindful of the words of his fatherly Paul which to this day may be seen as a valuable guideline for youngsters:[160]

"Let no man despise thy youth: but be thou an example of the faithful in word, in conversation, in charity, in faith, in chastity."

In fact, in reading through the various Epistles that Paul wrote, we see how the apostle liked to send our Saint as his representative to the various communities, like to the Corinthians, Philippians, and Colossians,[161] clearly trusting in Timothy's soft-spoken, gentle way to exhort the faithful to remain firm in the Faith no matter what hardships they faced—and would feel greatly comforted as his beloved son in faith would aways return with a good report that the brethren had remained beholden to Christ's teachings.

Furthermore, our Saint played a vital role in the Early Church, and was a prominent figure in helping to spread Christianity throughout the Roman Empire. He became known for his dedica-

---

160 I Tim. 4:12.

161 I Cor. 4:17 and 16:10; II Cor. 1:19; Phil. 1:1 and 2:19; Col. 1:1.

tion to Christ's gospel message; his diligence in conducting his pastoral duties in a kind and gentle way; his unselfish concern for others in his firm commitment to the well-being of all who came under his care—all of which may be seen as having set our dear Timothy on the path of holiness leading him into the realms of sainthood, and inspiring all those seeking to enter into the religious life to follow his saintly example.

Saint Paul
(c. 5 AD—c. 67/68 AD)

CHAPTER 5

Saint Paul

June 30

Saint Paul (born Saul) became an important leader of the Early Church his stalwart determination to persevere in the Faith (even when faced with persecution on many occasions) eventually earning him a holy martyrdom (believed to have occurred around 67/68 AD).

While we know not the exact date of our Saint's birth, historical records depict it to have been around 5 AD in the Roman city of Tarsus in the province of Cilicia (modern-day Turkey), where he was born into a family of strict Pharisees.

In keeping with the Pharisaical thinking of the times, prior to his conversion, Saul was passionate in defending the Jewish law and traditions. Once he heard of Jesus, he refused to accept that this Man from Nazareth had come into the world as the long-awaited Messiah (replacing the old sacrificial covenant God made with Abraham with a new and eternal covenant through the sacrificial outpouring of His own blood to atone for mankind's sins). In his blind zeal to defend the Mosaic law, Saul traveled to Jerusalem and began persecuting the Christians—not only consenting to the stoning of dear Stephen[162] but thereafter going from house to house arresting both men and

[162] Acts 7:57 and 22:19-20.

women, and committing them to prison.[163] But as Our Lord had a different plan for Saul, He gave him a miraculous awakening[164]—which, as is well known, happened when the young persecutor of Christians was traveling from Jerusalem to Damascus (armed with letters from the high priest addressed to the various synagogues, demanding that if any Christian be found in that city they were to be arrested so that Saul could take them back to Jerusalem).

While traveling along the highway with his comrades, all united in their wicked cause, Saul was suddenly blinded by an unusually brilliant light. It was so intense that he fell to his knees, unable to progress any further as he was left completely in darkness. At the same time, he heard a heavenly voice calling to him:

"*Saul, Saul, why persecutest thou Me?*"

Unable to see, and not recognizing the voice, but already feeling fearful, Saul cried out:

"*Who art thou, Lord?*"

The wondrous voice continued:

"*I am Jesus whom thou persecutest.*"

His entire body now trembling, Saul humbly murmured:

"*Lord, what wilt Thou have me do?*"

At this, Jesus told him to rise and go into the city where it would be revealed to him.

Now the men who accompanied Saul were similarly fearful for although they could hear a voice, they could see no-one. They helped Saul to his feet (for he was completely blind) and guided him along the rest of the way. But already Saul was filled with a deep sense of remorse on discovering that the wondrous voice was that of Jesus of Nazareth (whose followers he had been persecuting)—and on arrival in Damascus, for three days he went on a strict fast,[165]

---

[163] Acts 8:3.
[164] Acts 9:1-8.
[165] Acts 9:9.

anxious to make reparation for his having committed what he now realized was an extremely grave and mortal sin.

On the third day, a holy man named Ananias received a vision of Jesus telling him to go to the house of Saul and heal him of his blindness,[166] for Jesus had elected this persecutor of Christians to preach His holy Name "*before the Gentiles, and kings, and the children of Israel.*" Amazed to hear of this incredible conversion of a man well known for his cruelty to Christians, with great faith the saintly Ananias hurried to the house where Saul was staying, and after laying his hands on him, healed him of his blindness—and also baptized him.

From thenceforward, Saul was a different man (as time went on, becoming known as the apostle Paul). Indeed, promptly after Ananias left him, he went into the various synagogues in Damascus, boldly declaring that Jesus Christ is the Son of God[167]—his words confounding the Jews, who muttered among themselves:

"*Is not this he who persecuted in Jerusalem those that called upon this name: and came hither for that intent, that he might carry them bound to the chief priests?*"

But Paul ignored their mutterings, increasing all the more in strength and determination. In due time, however, the confounded Jews sought to kill him[168]—but thanks to divine intervention, the local Christians helped him to escape under cover of darkness (by letting him down in a basket through one of the windows in the outer walls of the city).

Thereafter, Paul withdrew into the Arabian desert[169] and is believed to have spent some time on Mount Sinai where, like what happened to Moses, it appears that the Word of God was revealed to him—as later indicated in Paul's Epistle to the Galatians:[170]

---

166 Acts 9:10-18.
167 Acts 9:20-22.
168 Acts 9:23-25.
169 Gal. 1:17.
170 Gal. 1:11-12.

"For I give you to understand, brethren, that the gospel which was preached by me is not according to man. For neither did I receive it of man, nor did I learn it; but by the revelation of Jesus Christ."

After his solitary time in the desert, Paul stalwartly returned to Damascus, where he remained for a while until, almost three years having passed since his conversion, he then traveled to Jerusalem—hoping to join the disciples in their holy crusade.[171] But in light of Paul's earlier reputation, the brethren were understandably skeptical—all but dear Barnabas who felt guided by the Holy Ghost to introduce the converted Paul to Peter; and indeed in his typically kind and consoling way, Barnabas was able to convince Peter to accept Paul as a genuine convert. So Christ's chosen Prince of the Apostles met with Paul over a period of fifteen days[172] (although not with the other Apostles at this time, but only James the Just).[173] Thereafter, Peter assigned to our converted Saint the responsibility of conducting his life as a true apostle of Christ, preaching the Word of God, ordaining priests and even bishops.

In Jerusalem, however, as his preaching quickly met with opposition, the brethren sent Paul to Tarsus,[174] his hometown, where he stalwartly preached Christ's gospel message in this city of his birth, and right across Celicia for some ten years and more, until his kind and supportive friend Barnabas came to take him back to Antioch. Thereafter, we know that the two of them traveled together, bonded in their priestly brotherhood, preaching and converting over the many years of what became known as Paul's first missionary jour-

---

171 Acts 9:26-27.

172 Not, it appears, in the large home of Mark's mother, for it is believed that Paul never met Christ's holy Mother, not then nor when he returned to Jerusalem to prepare for the prophesied famine—by which time the Blessed Virgin Mary had already left the city to reside in Ephesus (where we know the Apostle John had a safe haven built for her on the outskirts of this city).

173 Gal. 1:18.

174 Acts 9:28-30.

ney—in spite of Paul continuing to face much persecution from the Jews.

Even throughout our Saint's second and third missionary journeys, working with Silas, Timothy, and Luke, he continued to suffer being scorned, threatened, and persecuted.

Not only did Paul suffer these many trials and tribulations but after his third missionary journey, he was made a prisoner for four years, commencing not long after he and Luke had left their beloved Timothy in Ephesus.

In studying what happened after their departure from Ephesus, the two of them first sailed into the Roman province of Syria, stopping off in Tyre for seven days (as their ship was scheduled to unload its cargo here).[175] In this seaport, certain disciples warned Paul not to return to Jerusalem as they believed his life would be in danger. However, as our valiant Saint felt called by Christ to accept whatever God willed for him—and his faithful friend Luke refused to abandon him—before their departure, their disciple friends and families knelt on the seashore and prayed together for God to protect and guide them[176] (similar to what happened before Paul and Luke's departure from Ephesus).

They then set sail bound for Jerusalem, first stopping off in the seaport of Ptolemais in Phoenicia, and then progressing on to the harbor city of Caesarea[177] in Samaria. Once landed they stayed in the home of a disciple named Philip[178] (who like our saintly Stephen was one of the first seven deacons of the Early Church). He

[175] Acts 21:2-4.

[176] Acts 21:5-6.

[177] Also known as Caesarea Maritima (different from the inland city of Caesarea Philippi located near the foot of Mount Harmon in Syria; and from the inland city of Caesarea in the province of Cappadocia)—this particular Caesarea located on the coast in the Roman province of Samaria about sixty-five miles northwest of Jerusalem; originally an old, dilapidated town known as Strato's Tower, but later transformed by Herold the Great into a magnificent harbor city, which he renamed in honor of Caesar Augustus.

[178] Acts 21:8-9.

had four young daughters who also cautioned Paul not to travel to Jerusalem; their warning was confirmed a few days later[179] when a certain prophet named Agabus (who had just returned from Judea) warned Paul that in Jerusalem he would be arrested by the Jews and delivered into the hands of the Gentiles. However, our valiant Saint bravely responded:

"*The Will of the Lord be done.*"

And sure enough, after Paul and Luke's arrival in Jerusalem and Paul started preaching in the Temple—on the seventh day, Jews from Asia stirred up the people against him,[180] accusing him of violating the sacred grounds of the Temple by preaching a gospel that differed from their Jewish law (similar to what happened to Jesus; and to Stephen not long thereafter). The enraged mob laid hold of Paul, and after dragging him forth from the Temple would have killed him had it not been for the intervention of a Roman tribune,[181] Claudius Lysias, who after hearing that all of Jerusalem was in uproar, had promptly dispatched soldiers to bring Paul before him that he may determine what wrong he had done.

After learning more about him and discovering that our Saint was a Roman citizen, Lysias then ordered that Paul be sent under protected custody overland back to the harbor city of Caesarea[182]—as the city was governed by a Roman procurator named Felix.[183] (Given that Romans were typically classified as Gentiles, we are hereby drawn to see the prophecy of Agabus being fulfilled.) Determined not to abandon his dear friend, Luke followed the cohort from a distance.

---

179 Acts 21:10-14.

180 Acts 21:27-33.

181 High-ranking officer in the Roman army.

182 Acts 23:23-24.

183 Marcus Antonius Felix (born c. 5/10 AD, date of death unknown); fourth Roman procurator of Judea during 52–60 AD; known for his cruelty and his openness to bribery.

On their arrival in the city, Felix was handed a letter from the tribune which stated as follows:[184]

"*Claudius Lysias to the most excellent governor, Felix, greeting. This man being taken by the Jews, and ready to be killed by them, I rescued coming in with an army, understanding that he is a Roman: And meaning to know the cause which they objected unto him, I brought him forth into their council. Whom I found to be accused concerning questions of their law; but having nothing laid to his charge worthy of death or of bands. And when I was told of ambushes that they had prepared for him, I sent him to thee, signifying also to his accusers to plead before thee. Farewell.*"

After reading this letter (and in light of it being the Roman custom not to condemn any man without hearing both sides), Felix agreed to hear what Paul had to say once his accusers had arrived to present their case—and in the meantime, he ordered that Paul be kept as a prisoner in Herod's judgment hall.[185]

Five days later when the high priest Ananias arrived in Caesarea from Jerusalem, accompanied by some of the ancients and their orator named Tertullus, Felix had Paul brought before them so that he could hear both sides.[186] After listening to Tertullus, the governor then permitted our Saint to speak, whereupon Paul presented a most convincing case in his own defense against the orator's accusations—so much so that Felix had no choice but to dismiss Paul's accusers. Yet even so, he continued to keep Paul as a prisoner under the care of a centurion, while allowing him to have visitors (during which time Luke was able to remain in contact with his friend).

Now in the early days of Paul's imprisonment we note that on at least one occasion Felix summoned our Saint to appear before

---

184 Acts 23:26-30.

185 Acts 23:33-35. This King Herod being Agrippa II, son of Agrippa I.

186 Acts 24:1-23.

him—as his wife Drusilla[187] (who happened to be a Jew) wanted to hear about the Christian Faith. So Paul, in his usual stalwart way, preached to them about the Word of God—but once he spoke of chastity, divine justice and the judgment to come, Felix became very fearful, and refused to hear any more.[188] Instead, during Paul's time of confinement he called on him periodically, seeking a bribe (something this governor was prone to do)—a request that our Saint never gave into. As a result Paul ended up being held in custody for two years in Caesarea before Felix was succeeded by a new governor.[189]

Once this new governor, Portius Festus,[190] took over from Felix, after his initial three days in Caesarea, he traveled to Jerusalem—where he was promptly faced with the enraged grumblings of the chief priests and other Jewish men of authority who wanted Paul returned to Jerusalem.[191] Festus, however, told them that as the prisoner was already held in Caesarea, if any man had a grievance against him, they were to accompany him back to the city and present their case before him. He then tarried in Jerusalem some eight or ten days before traveling back to Caesarea—where, the very next day he summoned both Paul and his accusers that he may hear both sides as he sat on his judgment chair.

After the Jews presented their many grievances against Paul (demanding again that he be returned to Jerusalem for judgment), Festus turned to Paul and asked if he would be willing to go back to the

---

187 Felix is believed to have married three times, although historical records reveal no information as to his third wife. His first wife was Drusilla of Mauretania, probably the daughter of Ptolemy of Mauretania and Julia Urania. Felix's second wife (a divorcee) was this Drusilla of Judea, daughter of Herod Agrippa I and Cypros.

188 Acts 24:24-25.

189 Acts 24:26-27.

190 Portius Festus, fifth Roman procurator of Judea (c. 60–62 AD), succeeding Antonius Felix somewhere between 55–60 AD. History describes him as fair and reasonable—much more so than Felix or Festus' successor, Albinus.

191 Acts 25:1-6.

city and defend himself before the Jews.[192] But having already faced near-death in Jerusalem, our Saint was understandably suspicious that this was merely a ruse for the Jews to kill him on the way. So he appealed to the governor that as a Roman citizen he be allowed to go to Rome to present his case before Caesar.[193] After a brief consult with his council, Festus then told Paul:

"*To Caesar shalt thou go.*"

However, before allowing his prisoner to board a ship bound for Rome, it so happened that King Agrippa II[194] (along with his sister Bernice) arrived in Caesarea to salute Festus as the new governor.[195] Still somewhat troubled and anxious for a second opinion, Festus shared with the king the difficult situation with which he was faced regarding this prisoner that he had inherited from his predecessor; whereupon the king agreed that he would hear what Paul had to say. So the next day, King Agrippa and Bernice (with much pomp and splendor) entered the judgment hall, where Festus, accompanied by a number of tribunes and principal men of the city were already gathered.[196] Having summoned Paul, Festus then publicly presented his case before the king:

"*King Agrippa, and all ye men who are here present with us, you see this man, about whom all the multitude of the Jews dealt with me at Jerusalem, requesting and crying out that he ought not to live any longer. Yet have I found nothing that he hath committed worthy of death. But forasmuch as he himself hath appealed to Augustus, I have determined to send him.*"

---

192 Acts 25:7-9.

193 Acts 25:10-12.

194 Marcus Julius Agrippa II (c. 27/28–c. 92/100 AD), last ruler from the Herodian dynasty reigning over territories outside of Judea as a Roman client.

195 Acts 25:13-22.

196 Acts 25:23-27.

And he asked King Agrippa to recommend what charges could be laid against his prisoner before sending him to Rome to be judged by Caesar Augustus[197] (also known as Emperor Nero).

Turning to our Saint, the king then ordered him to speak.[198] So Paul spoke at some length, in his typical way persevering in the Faith.[199] He first shared with the king and his audience his miraculous conversion on the way to Damascus, and then went on to preach about Christ's Kingdom; whereupon King Agrippa told our Saint:

"*In a little thou persuadest me to become a Christian!*"

The king, his sister, and Festus then stepped aside to discuss the situation, whereupon all three of them agreed that they believed Paul had done nothing that warranted a death sentence.[200] In fact, King Agrippa said to Festus:

"*This man might have been set at liberty, if he had not appealed to Caesar.*"

So as a prisoner (under a centurion named Julius), Paul was placed on board a ship bound for Rome[201]—whereupon Luke (who had been following all that had transpired) promptly boarded the same ship and remained with Paul throughout this time. The two of them faced many trials for their journey ended up a most arduous one.[202] Their ship was attacked by high winds and violent storms, especially after leaving Crete. As author of the Acts of the Apostles, in his recording of the event Luke explains that Paul comforted all who were with them, sharing with them that an angel of God had

---

197 Nero Claudius Caesar Augustus Germanicus (Dec. 15, 37 AD–June 9, 68 AD), also known as Emperor Nero and/or Caesar Augustus; fifth Roman Emperor and final emperor of the Julio-Claudian dynasty, reigning from 54 AD until his death in 68 AD.

198 Acts 26:1.

199 Acts 26:2-28.

200 Acts 26:30-32.

201 Acts 27:1-2.

202 Acts 27:14-25.

appeared before him, telling him that all would be saved.[203] And sure enough, in spite of their ship running aground (at which point the soldiers on board wanted Paul and the other prisoners killed to ensure they wouldn't escape), the centurion Julius (who liked and respected Paul) conversely ordered that all were free to swim ashore—whereupon, as the angel of God had promised, all made it safely to the island of Melita.[204]

During their three month stay on this island, when a snake (a viper) bit our Saint's hand which required no healing, Luke describes how the local barbarians saw Paul as a man of God, and promptly converted.[205] Furthermore, when he healed a very sick man of his illness, they brought all their sick and ailing to their beloved Paul—and he promptly healed them all.[206]

Once their ship was ready, Paul and his dear friend Luke then set sail for Rome—and having finally arrived in the city, our Saint was placed under house arrest with a soldier that kept him under guard. Come the third day, no doubt somewhat perplexed that he had not been summoned to appear before Caesar, Paul requested that the chiefs among the local Jews be allowed to visit with him[207]—and once they assembled in his house, he appealed to them, saying:

"*Men, brethren, I, having done nothing against the people, or the custom of our fathers, was delivered prisoner from Jerusalem into the hands of the Romans; who, when they had examined me, would have released me, for that there was no cause of death in me; But the Jews contradicting it, I was constrained to appeal unto Caesar; not that I had any thing to accuse my nation of. For this cause therefore I desired to see you, and to speak to you. Because that for the hope of Israel, I am bound with this chain.*"

203 Acts 27:22-24.
204 Lk. 27:41-44.
205 Acts 28:3-6.
206 Acts 28:8-9.
207 Acts 28:16-20.

But the Jews said to him:[208]

"*We neither received letters concerning thee from Judea, neither did any of the brethren that came hither, relate or speak any evil of thee. But we desire to hear of thee what thou thinkest; for as concerning this sect, we know that it is everywhere contradicted.*"

So a day having been appointed, a great number came to the house and Paul stalwartly preached to them from morning to night, giving testimony to the Kingdom of God through the presence of Christ who, he explained came not to subvert their Mosaic law, but rather to fulfill it.[209] Once again, it seems that some believed and converted while others walked away, still not convinced. Even so, it would appear that none reported our Saint to Caesar.

As a result, we see that Paul ended up being a housebound prisoner for a further two years,[210] stalwartly preaching Christ's gospel to all who came and visited with him (during which time it is believed that Paul wrote three of his Epistles[211]). And throughout this time, his good friend Luke remained his faithful companion—joined a little later by their beloved Timothy after he had received Paul's letter, begging him to come to him (as previously mentioned).

Eventually, as our Saint had still not been ordered to appear before Caesar, the Jews decided to release him. So the three friends then parted company (Luke to preach elsewhere and Timothy to return to Ephesus) while Paul set forth to accomplish his fourth missionary journey—first traveling to the island of Crete, then to Nicopolis, and then, as had been his long-time intention, to Spain for a brief visit[212] (as confirmed by certain Christian writers[213]).

---

208 Acts 28:21-22.

209 Acts 28:23-24.

210 Acts 28:30-31.

211 To the Ephesians, the Colossians and the Philippians.

212 Romans 15:24 and 28.

213 Pope Clement I (bishop of Rome from 88–99 AD and one of the earliest Early Church Fathers); St. John Chrysostom (c. 347–Sept. 14, 407); Cyril of Jerusalem (c. 313–386).

He then returned to Rome to work alongside his Apostle friend Peter (which turned out to be our Saint's fifth and last missionary journey).[214] For not long after his arrival, the Great Fire of 64 AD broke out, rumored to have been caused by Emperor Nero (the same previously mentioned Caesar Augustus) in his bid to raze a large portion of the city so that he could have a new palace built.[215] (In fact, one historian known as Tacitus[216] claimed that as a youngster, he saw the Emperor merrily playing a fiddle while his city went up in flames). Unable to dispel the rumors and anxious to divert fault away from himself, Nero blamed the devastation on what he called a rebellious cult (the Christians)—and in order to prove his point, began persecuting them. He first had their leader Peter arrested, and then Paul later that same day.

According to Tradition, they were both cast into a dank, dark, foul-smelling dungeon in the infamous Mamertine Prison in Rome, where they remained for some years until Nero had them brought forth for sentencing (believed to have been c. 67/68 AD).

While we know that Peter was crucified (upside down as he refused to be crucified the same way as his divine Master)—as Paul was a Roman citizen, Nero had him beheaded (a method of execution allowed citizens of the Roman Empire); both Peter and Paul said to have been martyred on the same day in what was known as the Neronian Gardens where the Emperor was enacting his gruesome persecutions.

---

214 During this time, we remember that Mark made a short visit to Rome to be with his beloved Peter—no doubt pleased to have a chance to reconnect with Paul.

215 The Great Fire of Rome began on July 18, 64 AD in the enormous Circus Maximus stadium, and burned for six days before being brought under control. However, the fire then reignited and burned for another three days, destroying a large segment of the city.

216 Publius Cornelius Tacitus, simply known as Tacitus (c. 56 AD–c. 120 AD); a Roman historian and politician, widely regarded as one of the greatest Roman historians by modern scholars.

Further belief dictates that they were both buried in the close vicinity of these gardens—at the foot of the Vatican Hill.[217] Eventually their relics were transferred to two major basilicas built in their honor in Rome—those of the Prince of the Apostles placed under the high altar of St. Peter's Basilica, and those of our Saint placed beneath a marble tombstone (bearing the Latin inscription "*Paulo Apostolo Mart*") in the crypt of the Basilica of St. Paul Outside the Walls.

After Christ touched St. Paul's sinful soul he became an outstanding apostle and a prominent leader in the early Christian world as he stalwartly persevered in the Faith—in spite of being scorned, threatened and persecuted on a vast number of occasions.

Indeed, in his Second Epistle to the Corinthians,[218] we find an alarming description of all that our saintly Paul endured:

"*Of the Jews five times did I receive forty stripes, save one. Thrice was I beaten with rods, once I was stoned, thrice I suffered shipwreck, a night and a day I was in the depth of the sea. In journeying often, in perils of waters, in perils of robbers, in perils from my own nation, in perils from the Gentiles, in perils in the city, in perils in the wilderness, in perils in the sea, in perils from false brethren. In labour and painfulness, in much watchings, in hunger and thirst, in fastings often, in cold and nakedness.*"

May our beloved Paul's bold perseverance in the face of all these hardships and sufferings, inspire us to valiantly soldier on throughout the challenges of our own pilgrim journey to Heaven.

Furthermore, to help us in our daily battles, we have our Saint's many Epistles (occupying a large portion of the New Testament) which continue to have an influential impact on the Christian world today; in their own way providing valuable reminders to persevere

---

[217] Vatican Hill—a hill in Rome, located on the right bank of the Tiber river, opposite the traditional seven hills of Rome.

[218] II Cor. 11:24-27.

in the one true Faith—and never give in to those who preach a different gospel from that of our Lord and Savior, Jesus Christ.

Saint Luke
(c. 9 AD—84 AD)

CHAPTER 6

Saint Luke

October 18

Saint Luke, in his determination to remain with his dear friend Paul throughout the years of his confinement, was clearly blessed with a most kind and compassionate heart—like the good Samaritan described in one of Christ's parables. Not only was Luke gifted this way, but Tradition dictates that he became an outstanding Early Christian and was considered among the most cultured members of the Early Church—ultimately suffering a holy martyrdom in the year 84 AD at the hands of a pagan mob (like what happened to his good friend Timothy).

Historical records reveal that our Saint was born around 9 AD in the Greek city of Antioch, where he grew up and became a physician.[219] While we have no information as to when he became a convert, it may well have happened shortly after Stephen's martyrdom when the Apostles sent their initial disciples away from Jerusalem—some who were Greek-speaking arriving in Luke's hometown and preaching the Word of God, which we know was joyfully received by the Gentiles.[220] However, before Barnabas' arrival in Antioch, it would seem that shortly after Luke's conversion, he left his hometown and traveled to Jerusalem, where he knew the Apostles were

---

219 Col. 4:14.

220 Acts 11:19-22.

based at the time. For in light of Luke becoming an evangelist, commencing his holy Gospel with information about Christ's holy Mother, we are drawn to believe that he must have known and loved the Blessed Virgin Mary—his close association and devotion to her enabling him to include a number of interesting details in his evangelical writing, not found in the other Gospels.

Furthermore, in light of his close association with the Apostles and various members of the Christian community, he was clearly guided by the Holy Ghost to write his Acts of the Apostles—providing a brief history of the first thirty years of the Early Church after Christ's Ascension. Yet in spite of his close involvement with the Early Church, in reviewing the Acts we note that the only reference to Luke's presence is when he worked with Paul and his companions, at which time rather than referring to himself by name he uses the pronoun "*we*"—drawing us to realize that not only was our Saint gifted with compassion, but also the holy virtue of humility.

Turning now to the interesting details found in Luke's Gospel, we find a beautiful description of the Annunciation,[221] followed by the Virgin Mary's Visitation to her elderly cousin Elizabeth in the city of Juda[222] (where Luke includes the prophecy of Zachary that his child John the Baptist would become a great prophet; one who would prepare the way for the coming of Jesus Christ, our Savior, "*the horn of Salvation*").[223] Our Saint then goes on to enthrall us with the Birth of Jesus in a lowly stable on the outskirts of Bethlehem,[224] followed by the shepherds' visit to Mary and Joseph where they find the Baby Jesus wrapped in swaddling clothes and lying in a manger, just as told to them by an angel.[225]

---

221 Lk. 1:26-38.
222 Lk. 1:39-65.
223 Luke 1:67-77.
224 Lk. 2:4-7.
225 Lk. 2:8-16.

After his joyful sharing, in his compassionate way Luke outlines a number of events that would have brought great sorrow to Christ's holy Mother, to include an insightful description of Simeon's woeful prediction to Mary when she and Joseph had taken the Baby Jesus into the Temple for His Presentation:[226]

"*Behold this Child is set for the fall, and for the resurrection of many in Israel, and for a sign which shall be contradicted. And thy own soul a sword shall pierce, that, out of many hearts, thoughts may be revealed.*"

Similarly, our Saint describes Mary's great sorrow on discovering that her twelve-year old Jesus had remained behind in Jerusalem when the traveling caravans had departed for their hometown of Nazareth (on the third day Mary and Joseph finding Him in the Temple where Jesus was amazing the learned doctors with His wisdom at such a young age).[227] Thereafter, Luke tells us that the Holy Family returned to their hometown of Nazareth where "*Jesus advanced in wisdom, and age, and grace with God and men.*"[228]

Our Saint's next chapter jumps forward in time to John the Baptist coming forth from the desert and preaching "*the baptism of penance for the remission of sins;*"[229] telling the people that while he was baptizing with water, "*there shall come One mightier than I, the latchet of Whose shoes I am not worthy to loose: He shall baptize you with the Holy Ghost, and with fire.*" [230] And sure enough, Jesus (now a young man of thirty) then appears[231] and as is well known, prior to commencing His divine ministry, is baptized in the River Jordan by John the Baptist, where Luke tells us that the heavens were opened and "*the Holy Ghost descended in a bodily shape, as a dove upon Him;*

---

226 Luke 2:22-35.
227 Luke 2:42-47.
228 Luke 2:51-52.
229 Luke 3:1-3.
230 Luke 3:16.
231 Luke 3:21-22.

and a voice came from Heaven: Thou art my beloved Son; in Thee I am well pleased."

Over time Luke must have learned about Christ's many valuable teachings from the Blessed Virgin Mary, Apostles and disciples, for he covers a good number of them in his following chapters (to include Christ's lengthy Sermon on the Mount).[232]

Furthermore, as a physician (no doubt amazed over Christ's miraculous healings) Luke also describes a large number of Christ's miracles—like Our Lord's healing a man of his leprosy, and another with palsy;[233] His healing a man with a withered hand, and the sick servant of a centurion;[234] His healing a woman who was completely buckled over for eighteen years, and a man with dropsy;[235] His healing ten lepers, followed by His healing of a blind beggar man.[236] Included among these miraculous healings, Luke also describes Christ's restoring to life a widow's son on the outskirts of the city of Naim,[237] and the daughter of Jairus, a ruler of the local synagogue.[238]

We can readily ascertain from our Saint's writings that as both a writer and a doctor, he sought to help all those in need of healing by drawing attention to the power of Christ's healing love. Furthermore, that all may experience the joy of Christ's love, Luke draws attention to that which we must first aim to do, by his quoting the words of the First Commandment:[239] "*Thou shalt love the Lord thy God with thy whole heart, and with thy whole soul, and with all thy strength, and with all thy mind: and thy neighbour as thyself.*"

---

232 Lk. 6:20-49.
233 Lk. 5:12-13; 5:18-25;.
234 Luke 6:6-10; 7:2-10.
235 Luke 13:11-13; 14:1-4.
236 Lk. 17:12-14; 18:35-42.
237 Lk. 7:11-15.
238 Lk. 8:41; 49-50.
239 Lk. 10:27.

That we may gain a better understanding of who our neighbor is, our Saint goes on to share Christ's valuable explanation of its meaning—as found in His parable on the good Samaritan,[240] who was traveling along the highway when he came upon a man who had been attacked by robbers, stripped and left half-dead by the wayside. With tender compassion, this good Samaritan pauses his travels to help this complete stranger, and having tendered to his wounds, he sets the injured man upon his beast and brings him to an inn that he may be taken care of.

To further expound upon the meaning of compassion, Luke shares Christ's parable on the prodigal son,[241] who after regretting his dissolute living returns home, a humble penitent, and is promptly forgiven. Luke also describes Christ's parable pertaining to Lazarus,[242] a poor man who was covered in sores and would beg for crumbs from the rich man's table without success; but when he died was rewarded by entering into the joy of Heaven—unlike the rich man who lacked compassion, refusing to give to Lazarus and others in need, and "*was buried in hell.*"

Having covered the joy of Christ's preachings and healings, our Saint tells the sad story of Satan entering into the heart of Judas Iscariot, prompting him to betray Our Lord to the chief priests and magistrates who had been seeking how they might secretly put Jesus away on the feast of the upcoming Pasch.[243]

And a plan having been set in place, Luke describes how Jesus, full knowing what Judas was about to do, after His Last Supper took His Eleven to a place on the mount of Olives where they would often go to pray.[244] And here, our Saint goes on to explain that Jesus suffered a terrible spiritual agony—whereupon the Eternal Father

---

[240] Lk. 10:30-35.
[241] Lk. 15:11-32.
[242] Lk. 16:20-22.
[243] Lk. 22:1-6.
[244] Lk. 22:39-44.

sent down an angel to comfort and strengthen His beloved Son for "*His sweat became as drops of blood, trickling down upon the ground.*"

Shortly thereafter, Judas then appears accompanied by a great multitude—and as is well known, betrays Our Lord with a kiss,[245] which led to Jesus being apprehended and taken to the house of the high priest, where He was blasphemously mocked and treated with savage cruelty throughout the night; the next morning then taken before Pontius Pilate for sentencing.

In his next chapter, Luke quotes Pilate's words to the chief priests, magistrates and people, indicating his difficulty in knowing what to do with Jesus:[246]

"*You have presented unto me this man, as one that perverteth the people; and behold I, having examined him before you, find no cause in this man, in those things wherein you accuse him. No, nor Herod neither. For I sent you to him, and behold, nothing worthy of death is done to him. I will chastise him therefore, and release him.*"

However, we know that Pilate, being faced with violent opposition from the chief priests, magistrates and miscreants (who continued to scream for Christ's crucifixion) ultimately surrenders to their vicious demands and condemns Jesus to death[247]—while releasing a man imprisoned for murder and sedition[248] (it being the standard practice to release a prisoner at this time of the Jewish Pasch).

No doubt himself deeply grieved while sharing the above, our Saint then describes how a foreigner named Simon (who was from Cyrene in Libya, Africa) was called upon to help Jesus carry His heavy Cross,[249] and goes on to describe how Jesus at some point along the way of His torturous walk to Calvary turned to the women

245 Lk. 22:47-66.
246 Lk. 23:14-16.
247 Lk. 23:24.
248 Lk. 23:25.
249 Lk. 23:26.

who were following (bewailing and lamenting Him), telling them gently but firmly:[250]

"*Daughters of Jerusalem, weep not over Me; but weep for yourselves, and for your children.*"

Then once Jesus arrives on Calvary's hilltop—that all may know of the infinite mercy of our Lord and Savior—Luke tells how Jesus, while being nailed to the Cross, cried out to His Father in Heaven:[251]

"*Father, forgive them, for they know not what they do.*"

Clearly amazed over Christ's loving mercy, our saintly Luke goes on to further share what happened after an exchange of words between the two crucified robbers hanging one on either side of Jesus.[252] While the one called out, "*If thou be Christ, save thyself and us,*" the other rebuked him, saying:

"*Neither dost thou fear God, seeing thou art condemned under the same condemnation? And we indeed justly, for we receive the due reward of our deeds; but this Man hath done no evil.*"

And turning to Jesus, he humbly begged of Him,

"*Lord, remember me when Thou shalt come into Thy Kingdom.*"

Here, Luke rejoicingly tells us that our merciful Lord and Savior promptly forgave this penitent sinner, telling him:[253]

"*Amen I say to thee, this day thou shalt be with Me in Paradise.*"[254]

Continuing Luke's account of what happened on Calvary's hilltop that day,[255] shortly after this event, at the sixth hour darkness

---

[250] Lk. 23:28.

[251] Lk. 23:34.

[252] Lk. 23:39-42.

[253] Lk. 23:43.

[254] This Paradise being the happy state of everlasting rest, joy, and peace that Christ was pleased, by a special privilege, to reward the faith and confession of this penitent thief, with a full discharge of all his sins, both as to the guilt and punishment; and to introduce him immediately after death into the happy society of the saints, whose Limbo, that is the place of their confinement, was now made a Paradise by Our Lord's going thither. [Scriptural note from the Douay-Rheims Bible].

[255] Lk. 23:44-45.

descended over the earth continuing until the ninth—when suddenly the veil of the Temple was ripped from top to bottom as Jesus cried out to His Father in Heaven:[256]

"*Father, into Thy Hands I commend My spirit.*"

And so saying, our beloved Savior gave up the ghost.

Determined to leave no detail out, our Saint tells us that the centurion watching over Jesus (overawed by what he saw and heard) promptly glorified God,[257] woefully professing:

"*Indeed this was a just man.*"

And all those who had remained in spite of the darkness now left Calvary's hilltop, humbly striking their breasts.

Throughout this time we know of course that Christ's holy Mother remained at the foot of the Cross with the Apostle John by her side—along with certain Holy Women (who had accompanied them along the way) standing close by.

Luke further reveals that they were joined by Joseph of Arimathea, a good and just man, who had gone to Pilate to beg that he be allowed to take down the Body of Jesus.[258] And having been granted permission, Joseph (together with John) take Jesus down from the Cross, and wrapping His Body in fine linens, laid Him in a sepulcher made of stone (one that had never been used before).[259]

Our Saint's final chapter then covers Christ's Resurrection and manifestation of Himself to His Apostles; his recounting providing some further interesting details in addition to that revealed by the other evangelists—commencing with the first day of the week (in biblical times) when certain of the Holy Women had gone to the

---

256 Lk. 23:46.

257 Lk. 23:47-48.

258 Lk. 23:49-53.

259 While not mentioned in Luke's Gospel, we know that John and Joseph of Arimathea gently placed the Body of Jesus in arms of His sorrowful Mother that she may tenderly embrace her beloved Son for the last time before they laid Him in the tomb.

tomb very early in the morning,[260] armed with spices to anoint the Body of Our Lord (for they did not understand Christ's words that on the third day He would rise again). As briefly mentioned previously, on their arrival our Saint tells us that they find the stone rolled back and as they stared at the opening, doubtless perplexed and troubled, they are approached by two angelic beings who confirmed that Jesus was no longer in His tomb but had risen, telling them:

"*Remember how He spoke unto you, when He was in Galilee, saying: The Son of Man must be delivered into the hands of sinful men, and be crucified, and the third day rise again.*"

When the women reported what they had seen and heard, we remember the Apostles were dumbfounded, such that Peter (accompanied by John at the time) ran to the tomb to see for himself what the women had revealed. Thereafter, Luke's Gospel provides us with the detailed account of the two disciples who, as previously mentioned, were walking along the highway about sixty furlongs from Jerusalem, when they were joined by a Stranger, who turned out to be their beloved Risen Christ.

Our Saint then goes on to describe Our Lord's miraculous appearance (in spite of the doors being locked for fear of the Jews) gently comforting all who were assembled in that large upper room in the house of Mark's mother, confirming that He had truly risen as He had said He would.[261] Thereafter, Luke ends this final chapter of his Gospel with Christ's promise that He would send the Holy Ghost to endow the Apostles "*with power from High*"[262] (which we know to have occurred at Pentecost), followed by just a brief reference to Christ's Ascension—after which all returned to Jerusalem filled with joy; thereafter frequently attending at the Temple, praising and thanking God.[263]

---

[260] Lk. 24:1-7.
[261] Lk. 24:36-48.
[262] Lk. 24:49.
[263] Lk. 24:50-53.

Given our Saint's compassionate nature, we can readily understand his desire to share with the world all that he had learned regarding the wondrous life of Jesus and His Blessed Virgin Mother, beginning with the Annunciation and ending with Christ's Ascension—his Gospel seen to cover a fairly extensive biography of their lives.

Indeed, in his devotion to Jesus and His holy Mother, in due time Luke became an artist (in fact, the founder of Christian iconography). He created a number of beautiful pictures of the Blessed Virgin Mary with the Child Jesus (believed to be seven in all)—one particular icon known by the title "*Salvation of the Roman People*" (the icon survives to this day in the Basilica of Santa Maria Maggiore in Rome).

Turning now to the Acts of the Apostles, we first find our Saint in the ancient Greek city of Troas where we know that he met up with Paul, Timothy and Silas. And after Paul was granted a vision during the night of a man beseeching them to come to Macedonia, from Luke's use of the word "*we,*" our Saint left Troas with Paul, Timothy and Silas bound for Philippi, where Paul and Silas were beaten with rods and thrown into prison after Paul had healed a girl with a demented spirit (as previously mentioned).

After Paul and Silas' miraculous release from prison, we know that the four of them parted company—Paul, Timothy, and Silas to continue their missionary travels, while Luke remained in Philippi, boldly determined to confirm the Faith in this vast Greek-speaking city. (Interestingly, over the six years that followed, we note that at no time does our Saint ever share with us the obvious success of his preaching and conversions—for such was the humble nature of our saintly Luke.)

Then when Paul and Timothy returned to Philippi to meet up with their dear friend, we remember that the three of them left together to travel back to Troas—where seven days later, our doctorly

Luke set sail with Timothy around the small peninsular to Assos (while Paul traveled the short distance overland). And once the three of them re-connected and set sail for Ephesus, as previously envisaged our kind and caring Luke was able to provide Paul with some helpful advice for their beloved Timothy (suggesting that he curtail his missionary travels to ease the discomfort of his serious abdominal medical problem). So once landed in Ephesus, after their three years of preaching in this city, we know that Paul altered saintly Timothy's missionary role by ordaining him as the first Bishop of Ephesus—before he and Luke left the city to commence their next missionary journey.

To expound upon what happened before Paul and Luke left Ephesus, in his typically kind and compassionate way, Luke describes how, after Paul had shared with the faithful that he suspected "*bands and afflictions*" awaited him in Jerusalem, "*there was much weeping among them all; and falling on the neck of Paul, they kissed him*" grieving that they may never see him again.[264]

Thereafter, our Saint provides us with a detailed description of their lengthy trip to Jerusalem—first sailing from Ephesus into the port of Coos. The following day they sailed to Rhodes, and from thence to Patara.[265] Having found a ship bound for Phenice, the two of them then sailed past Cyprus and into Syria, progressing on to Tyre.[266]

While their ship was unloading in this port, we know that they tarried for seven days with some Christian brethren who warned Paul not to go to Jerusalem—the following events then unfolding as covered in the previous chapter.

Now once Paul was released from his hired lodging in Rome, while he traveled to Crete (en route to Spain), Luke also left the

---

264 Acts 20:37-38.
265 Acts 21:1.
266 Acts 21:2-3.

city—eventually ending up in the Thebaid, a region in Ancient Egypt. While we have no details of his missionary work here, it is believed that Luke completed his Gospel and Acts of the Apostles during this time (finishing both before Paul's holy martyrdom).

Some time thereafter, Luke left the Thebaid and traveled to the city of Thebes in Boeotia (a region in Central Greece), where Tradition dictates that around the year 84 AD our seventy-five year old Saint was arrested by a pagan mob, viciously flayed alive, and then crucified on an olive tree.

According to a Greek historian, Nikephoros Kallistos Xanthopoulos,[267] our Saint's relics were later transferred from Thebes to Constantinople in 357, and at some point moved to Padua in Italy, where they remain to this day in the Basilica of Santa Giustina.

There is much we can learn from dear Saint Luke, for he was clearly influenced by the example of Christ's tender compassion—as seen not only in the way in which he accents on Christ's love and mercy in his Gospel, but also in his determination to remain with Paul throughout the time of his confinement.

Furthermore, we see how the humility of Christ's holy Mother also had an impact on our Saint's life, for he was very much a humble man—as seen in his Acts of the Apostles where (as previously mentioned) he never directs attention to himself by using his own name. Nor does he ever share any of his own healings or conversions.

May we too feel inspired to follow the example of our beloved Luke's saintly compassion in an imitation of Christ—and his virtuous gift of humility like that of Christ's lowly Virgin Mother.

---

267 Nikephoros Kallistos Xanthopoulos (c. 1256–1335), Greek ecclesiastical historian whose most popular work was the voluminous *Ecclesiastica Historia*, a significant documentary source on primitive Christianity and its doctrinal controversies.